CONVERSATIONS AT THE CASTLE

ARTS FESTIVAL OF ATLANTA

CONVERSATIONS AT THE CASTLE

CHANGING AUDIENCES AND CONTEMPORARY ART

Edited by
MARY JANE JACOB
With
MICHAEL BRENSON

THE MIT PRESS
CAMBRIDGE, MASSACHUSETTS   LONDON, ENGLAND

COVER:
The Castle, Atlanta, 1996 (exterior view)

ENDPAPERS:
The Castle (mezzanine, interior view)

FRONTISPIECE:
The Castle, 1996 (exterior view)

This book documents the exhibition program "Conversations at The Castle,"
organized by Mary Jane Jacob under the auspices of the **ARTS FESTIVAL OF ATLANTA**
and on public view from June 28 to September 29, 1996.

Printed and bound in Germany.

Library of Congress Cataloging-in-Publication Data

Conversations at the Castle: changing audiences and contemporary art/
    edited by Mary Jane Jacob with Michael Brenson.
        p.   cm.
    At head of title : Arts Festival of Atlanta.
    ISBN O-262-10072-X (hc : alk. paper)
    1. Arts Festival of Atlanta (1996 : Atlanta, Ga.)   2. Arts audiences—Georgia—Atlanta—Psychology.   3. Arts,
Modern—20th century—United States.   4. Arts, American.   I. Jacob, Mary Jane.   II. Brenson, Michael.   III. Arts
Festival of Atlanta (1996 : Atlanta, Ga.)
    NX427.A88C66   1998
    700'.1'0309758231—dc21   98-10767
                                                                                                           CIP

Table of Contents

In 1996 the Arts Festival of Atlanta embarked on a new path — a geographic move and an artistic leap. Begun in 1954, prompted by the need to expose and find a market for local artists, the Festival became a major annual city event, making its home the expansive grounds of beautiful Piedmont Park. As it grew, it continued the tradition of an artist's market but also offered exhibitions and performances, attracting a million and a half visitors in nine days. Increasingly, it pushed out, engaging other segments of the population with public artworks sited around the city.

In the decades since the Festival's founding, Atlanta has changed radically into a booming metropolis. We felt the urgency to both develop the Festival in a way that was consistent with the emerging world-class stature of our city — to help make Atlanta a cultural capital, too — while remaining devoted to our audience, a broad-based public constituency. We found that this transformation and maturing of the Festival, alongside that of the city itself, was not only an institutional concern for us but also a change endemic to the art field, which was feeling the need to serve a more democratic agenda called for by the National Endowment for the Arts during this period.

"Conversations at The Castle," during its organization and public phases, provided us with the occasion to think about who we were, to question how we relate to our audience, to reconceive what we can do, and to move ahead. Now, today, one year later, we are a part of the city, filling the streets of the downtown civic, business, and university center revitalized for the Olympics and adding to our program a wider scope of important performing and visual art from around the world. A physical re-siting, this is also a symbolic change. With the move out of a recreational park to an urban setting, the Festival pledges its commitment to bring together and demonstrate the compatibility of the various roles the arts can play — as entertainment and as an artistic or educational pursuit — within our daily lives and in the future of our community and its youth.

Three of our major and continuing sponsors joined us in presenting "Conversations at The Castle": AT&T, The Joseph B. Whitehead Foundation, and The Coca-Cola Company. Their grants were crucial to the realization of this program and at the same time signaled their support for the Festival's move toward timely and dramatic change. The support of the board of the Arts Festival of Atlanta was also an essential element in funding this program and our move toward change.

Initial planning funds for this program were received from Arts International, a division of the Institute for International Education. For this group of artists, an international network of funding agencies was put in place consisting of governmental and corporate entities that embraced the concept of commissioning, having the foresight to support the creation of these new works. We would like to thank for the Regina Frank project: Kade Collaborative Works Program, which is supported by the Annette Kade Endowment in memory of Max Kade; Arts International; Goethe-Institut/Atlanta; Senatsverwaltung fur Kulturelle Angelenheitan/Senate for Cultural Affairs, Berlin; Spiral/Wacoal Art Center, Tokyo; pixelpark, Berlin; InFocus Systems; Spectrum Data Systems; and IBM Interactive Media. Assistance for the IRWIN project was provided by: the Trust for Mutual Understanding, Soros Center for Contemporary Art, Ljubljana; Slovenian Ministry of Culture, Slovenian Information Office, City of Ljubljana; Sysen d.d., Mladina, Pristop d.d., and Hit d.d., Ljubljana; and Club Travel. Mauricio Dias and Walter Riedweg's work received funding from: Pro Helvetia/The Arts Council of Switzerland; CIBA Vision; Erziehungsdepartement Basel-Stadt Abteilung Kultur/Department of Education and Culture, City of Basel; and SWISSAIR. Ery Camara received a travel grant from Arts International, Maurice O'Connell from Arts Council/Aer Lingus Artflight Program, and artway of thinking from the Ministero degli Affari Esteri Italiano/Italian Ministry of Foreign Affairs, with additional cooperation for their project from the Italian companies de Majo/Vetreria in Murano, Illy Caffè, Nino Franco Spumanti, and Az. Vinicola Pagotta. This publication has been made possible with additional funding from The Nathan Cummings Foundation and Arts International.

—Patricia D. Gann
Executive Director
Arts Festival of Atlanta

Curator's Acknowledgments

Without a doubt "Conversations at The Castle" required the passion and dedication of many people. I would first like to thank my frequent collaborators: Rebecca DesMarais, who solely staffed an office at the Arts Festival of Atlanta for the first year, whose involvement and undauntedness was essential to making this idea a reality, and who, in her subsequent capacity as director of Youth Art Connection Gallery/Boys & Girls Clubs of Metro Atlanta, continued to work with many of the artists on their projects; Connie Baldwin, who served as development consultant, an increasingly challenging task that she accomplished with great professionalism, with grace, and with an appreciation of the goals the artists and myself hoped to accomplish; photographer John McWilliams, who contributed many of the fine images in this book and who brought into the project Chris Verene, whose particular view added much to capturing the scene and moment; and designer Lorraine Wild who, with her associate Amanda Washburn, so beautifully articulated our vision for this project in this book.

Architectural imagining and the demanding task of making the site of The Castle functional was the outstanding contribution of Merrill Elam of Scogin Elam and Bray Architects, Atlanta. Her involvement over many hours — in her office, at The Castle, and in city offices — along with the efforts of her assistants Jeff Atwood and Ned Frazer fulfilled a critical need. In carrying out these plans, I would like to thank Ted Stanuga, who coordinated the renovations along with Hank Bauer and his crew.

In January 1996 Julia Doran, a recent graduate of the University of Southern California's public art program, joined the staff as assistant curator, her qualifications including a healthy quotient of questioning the parameters of the field she was entering. She was the first among a group of students who formed the core of the production staff and whose similar sense of inquiry and dedication seemed to make them the most qualified assistants I could assemble. They were: Gabriela Fitz, Ana Teresa Prado Lopez, Susan Maruska, Anne Moore, and later in Chicago, Jeanne Hoel.

Maintaining the heart of the content and with a vision beyond the local scene, I was joined by Michael Brenson and Homi Bhabha who in March 1995 generously attended a brainstorming meeting in Chicago, where we were joined for this discussion by artists Alfredo Jaar and Ronald Jones. I was privileged to have Michael Brenson continue in the role of co-producer of "Conversations on Culture" and editor of the corresponding section of this book; it is the work of a great critic, a thinker about culture in our time, and a friend. Homi Bhabha's involvement as well has made this an occasion for the writing of an exceptionally insightful essay.

Finally I would like to thank Pat Gann, Lisa Tuttle, and the staff and board of directors of the Arts Festival of Atlanta for patiently and supportively allowing this project to develop and take place, and for all the many conversations we had.

—M. J. J.

FOREWORD
Lisa Tuttle

As I sit to write these comments, it is spring in Atlanta. Like most of my neighbors, I am engaged in a southeastern pastime and passion — gardening. Sitting on my front stoop in the early evenings, I contemplate the progress of my modest border garden. The irises need to be thinned; the lenten roses are finally filling in that bald spot. Cleome seedlings are sprouting everywhere but in the spot where I originally planted them. New plants such as a butterfly bush and lilies of the valley are arriving, selected from nurseries or catalogs. Old faithfuls — mostly transplants from the gardens of friends and family — are returning, producing additional "volunteers" that I can move to other areas in the garden.

Strategizing the programming of an annual arts festival and its trajectory of development is like the cultivation of a perennial garden. It is a seasonal process, with the garden's plants chosen for a

LISA TUTTLE has directed the visual arts programming of the Arts Festival of Atlanta since 1993. To this task she has brought an interdisciplinary approach, advocating hybridized art forms as a means to reach a wide range of viewers and bring together artists and audiences in new and energizing ways. For the Festival, she curated several exhibitions, often collaborating with other curators: "The Metaphorical Machine," "Money Changes Everything or Seeking the Soul" (with Xenia Zed), "Evidence of Performance" (with Rebecca Leary Safon), "Messages and Stories from the Everyday World" (with Jane Bickerton), and "Post-Olympia or How We Spent the Summer of 1996." She expanded the Festival's interdisciplinary and public art programming with "Art in Odd Places" and "City Site Works." An active participant in the contemporary art scene in Atlanta, Tuttle was gallery director for the Atlanta College of Art from 1986 to 1993 and for Nexus Contemporary Art Center from 1985 to 1986. As a practicing artist, she frequently exhibits her work, which includes video installation, performance, and objects. Tuttle received her BA in humanities and painting from New College in Sarasota, Florida, and also studied at the Atlanta College of Art and Georgia State University.

particular location and environment. Patience, experience, and vision, plus a certain element of boldness and experimentation, are required. Festivals, exhibitions, and programs are as time- or site-specific as works of art. Considering the environment, political climate, city, or institution for which they are fashioned reveals insight into the particular choices made. To understand why "Conversations at The Castle" counts among the most interesting programming hybrids that the Arts Festival of Atlanta has developed, offering much promise as the Festival moves toward the future, one must think about the time and site for which this exhibition program was developed.

A consideration of "Conversations" begins with an understanding of the scope of public art projects undertaken by the Arts Festival of Atlanta in the past, the role the Festival plays within the region's contemporary visual and performing arts community, the risks the Festival is willing to take with artists and curators, the trust of the Festival's large and diverse audiences, and the presence the Festival wished to have during the summer of 1996. These factors explain why Mary Jane Jacob was invited to develop a public art project at this time and, eventually (after months of curatorial discussion, artists' visits, fundraising, meetings, building codes, and program development), how "Conversations at The Castle" evolved into an exploration of an expanded concept of contemporary art in public space and modes of personal and cultural communication. This background, too, provides insight into the ways the Festival has grown, and will continue to flower, from these groundbreaking conversations.

For several years after the announcement that the Olympic Games were to be held in Atlanta, planning for the summer of 1996 was the constant focus of attention. Commercials proclaimed "The world is coming to Atlanta!" as a signboard over the downtown expressway counted down the days. The Olympics were perceived as Atlanta's — and the Festival's — opportunity for cultural attention and growth. The scramble to rise to the occasion seemed to permeate the city. Urban development and refurbishment were proposed. Attention to public art projects and their completion increased. The size and shape of the programming of the Cultural Olympiad and the eventual Olympic Arts Festival was a familiar topic of conversation. The Corporation for Olympic Development in Atlanta was formed to improve the quality of public spaces within the Olympic Ring — at the heart of which was created Centennial Park for the Olympics (p. 8) — and it issued several calls for artists to participate in public art and urban enhancement projects. The promise was "a legacy," leaving behind a culturally richer Atlanta as a benefit of the Games.

It was anticipated that in the summer of 1996 Atlanta would receive unprecedented international interest and numbers of visitors. There was much excitement among the arts community about this projected audience, and discussions about who would attend and the best ways to engage them abounded. Much effort was made in earnest to try to find the right exhibition or program to suit the occasion. There was the constant dilemma of a "regional" versus an "international" exhibition: should international artists be shown, or should we showcase regional artists to the world? Were we being disloyal to our southeastern artists if we exhibited artists from elsewhere, or was this a unique opportunity to have the resources to present international programming?

During this time, much like the city, the Arts Festival of Atlanta was experiencing a period of assessment, change, expansion, and growth. As an annual nine-day multidisciplinary festival presented each September, it featured both visual and performing arts, as well as a highly popular artist market. The Festival was and remains a well-loved local institution. As a community event, the Festival attracted a wide audience to its annual offerings in Piedmont Park, a 300-acre park in midtown Atlanta. But by the 1990s, the Festival was beginning to understand that it was outgrowing, both physically and philosophically, its traditional home. It began to seek a national, even international, presence. And like the cultural community around the Olympics, it questioned how it could develop in a larger arena and still serve its loyal hometown public.

For some who visited Atlanta for the first time during the Olympics, there were limited expectations of what could be produced here. Certainly there was little or no prior knowledge of the Arts Festival of Atlanta, the scope of its programming, and its history as a regional leader, particularly for its program of commissioned works in Piedmont Park beginning in 1981 with support from the National Endowment for the Arts.[1] In 1993, the Festival's public art program was renamed "City Site Works," and its concept moved from outdoor sculpture to more process-oriented, festival-as-site and city-as-site forms.[2] In the following two years these projects began to pave the way for the Festival's eventual departure from the park limits by engaging the urban environment, involving the community, and addressing social and historical issues concerning Atlanta's public spaces.[3]

In another interesting departure also initiated in 1993, the Festival's performing arts director, Rebecca Leary-Safon, and I began to see possibilities in creating linkages among the Festival's performance, visual arts, and educational programming. So as artworks moved further into the public realm, performance, too, came off the stage and onto the park grounds.[4] Finding sites, creating resources, cultivating and grafting constituencies, and following the evolving interests of the artists, the Festival began to collaborate with a variety of arts, grass-roots, educational, and social service organizations and to involve new participants in the programming. We began to understand more fully that public art, and festivals, could be perceived as creative forms of public service and that audiences could begin to find a sense of ownership and insight by participating in the artmaking process. Meanwhile, inviting visiting curators and co-curators contributed to an enriched environment and cross-pollination of programming and disciplines, mixing artists and elements of the city.[5]

1
Some of the artists who created works during this period of 1981 to 1992 were: Maria Artemis, James Casebere, Malcolm Cochran, Houston Conwill, Martin Emanuel, Scott Gilliam, Nade Haley, David Hammons, Maren Hassinger, Nene Humphrey, Mark Lere, Edward Levine, Donald Lipski, Marlene Malik, Larry Millard, Matt Mullican, Richard Nonas, Dennis Oppenheim, Richard Rezac, Kit-Yin Snyder, Meg Webster, and Frances Whitehead.

2
That year artist-curator Cesar Trasobares, who was responsible for renaming the program, selected Fred Wilson, Antonio Miralda, and Marilyn Gottlieb-Roberts to participate.

3
In 1994 the "City Site Works" selection committee of Trasobares, Patricia Fuller, and Stephanie Hughley selected Brad Brooks, Iñigo Manglano-Ovalle, Carl Pope, Sheila Kennedy/Juan Frano Violich, and Ritsuko Taho. Artists selected in 1995 were Jay Critchley, Peggy Diggs, Stephanie Johnson, REPOhistory, Lynne Yamamoto, and Aresh Javadi.

4
The trend toward site performances began with Japan's Theater Kataisha in 1993; "Evidence of Performance" with Janie Geiser, Sham Mosher, and Breath of the Earth, and Alyson Pou in 1994; and in 1995 Nia Love as part of the Environmental Performance Network presentations.

5
This direction included exhibitions such as: "The Language of Force" (1993), a show of ten artists examining violence in American cities, curated by Eddie Granderson; "Money Changes Everything or Seeking the Souk" (1994), curated by Xenia Zed and myself, which explored the relationship of visual arts exhibitions to the artists market; and "Messages and Stories from the Everyday World" (1995), curated by Jane Bickerton and myself, which relocated the exhibition site to billboards, the Internet, fax, and transit cards designed by artists.

These artistic programs paved the way for future change. In 1995, the board and staff of this forty-three-year-old organization, under the leadership of executive director Patricia D. Gann and board president Karen League, wrote a strategic plan that included a goal and vision for the year 2001. The Festival was to become "an internationally significant festival which presents challenging, innovative arts experiences in traditional and non-traditional settings. Building on a tradition of artistic excellence, we will increase collaborations with other organizations in an effort to be a continual force in building a cohesive and dynamic cultural ecology in Atlanta." As part of this new agenda, the Festival also aimed to bring art experiences traditionally deemed "high art" to its massive festival crowds, making them available and accessible on a popular level.

Many were concerned that the Festival would become unpopular and elitist if we pursued a dramatic change of programming and attempted to bring "challenging, innovative arts experiences" to a so-called "uninformed" broad general public. And this change and growth was being proposed within a popular, not-for-profit arts festival during the time of the national debate about public funding for the arts — the "culture wars." Without public funding, how could arts organizations continue to ensure the survival of their programs? Did the general public need or care about the arts? Artists, non-artists, arts administrators, critics, and curators talked of the need for artists and arts institutions to reconnect with their audiences, to bridge the seeming hostility. And, finally, as the notion of an "international" exhibition itself was being intensely debated on the larger cultural scene, what could be done in Atlanta that would enliven the international festival tradition rather than simply mimic a perhaps outmoded form? There were questions to be asked, conversations to be held.

All this brings us to the 1996 Festival, which became a constellation of events bridging the city and extending beyond the time of the Olympics. Instead of remaining in our September nine-day time slot, we began in June with a full four months of programming, of which "Conversations at The Castle" was a key part.[6] Looking back on that decision now, what a wise direction it was, though none of us were fully aware at the outset of the challenges and obstacles we would face with this venture. As the artists made their visits to Atlanta, they consistently and intelligently asked us questions about ourselves, Atlanta, the Olympics, the Festival, and the audience. For all of us — and for the Festival — these conversations were formative. The Arts Festival of Atlanta was launched into new arenas in all its areas of operation, and new standards were established as the program built upon the groundwork laid by the public art projects of preceding years.

Some visitors came to "Conversations at The Castle" because of their interest in the artists' projects; others because of the lure of the atmosphere of the Olympic Games. Atlanta participants came to the exhibition and the discussions with a wide range of expectations. My personal memories of the conversations I attended are vivid because each was so lively and so different. At one of the first discussions arranged by IRWIN — surrounded by an animated and agitated group of Slovenians, Russians, Germans, Brazilians, Senegalese, Americans, Swiss, Irish, and

6
The Festival's annual public art program continued with "Art in Odd Places," a site-specific sculpture exhibition of twenty-three Georgia artists' projects, conceived by artists Donna Pickens and Mari-anne Weinberg-Benson through the Individual Visual Artists Coalition. Along with "Conversations at The Castle," these projects were featured in the Cultural Olympiad's map of the seventy public art projects in Atlanta occasioned by the Olympics.

Other summer 1996 Festival programs were: Eiko and Koma's site performance "River" and "Survival Arts/Free Zone for Artists," a collaboration with 7 Stages Theatre, which focused on work from the former Yugoslavia.

In September, at the traditional time of the Festival, a series of visual and performing arts projects entitled "Post-Olympia, or How We Spent the Summer of 1996," focused on Atlanta artists' response to the summer's events.

others discussing art, politics, nationalism, and aesthetics — I realized that a change was occurring. At another conversation, this time on contemporary art and institutions, the artists, arts administrators, public art consultants, critics, and curators assembled were asked to identify one obstacle we faced each day in our work. One by one, the members of this diverse but articulate group voiced their concerns. For myself, as both an artist and a curator, I felt challenged as an arts administrator to sustain the level of excitement and sense of accomplishment that I gain from my work as an artist.[7]

It is my belief that the festival format can allow the kind of curatorial as well as artistic creativity that allows ideas, such as "Conversations at The Castle," to be played out in new ways. Ultimately, what the Festival carries forward from this important endeavor are a number of elements to be cultivated. Certainly, there is a large group of artists, critics, and art workers from all over the world that has a new familiarity and relationship with the Arts Festival of Atlanta. One significant development is a new confidence that this Festival is capable of sustaining growth and change, grafting international aspects onto its programming without jettisoning cherished elements.

In 1997, the Festival transplants itself — leaving its traditional home in Piedmont Park and moving downtown. Its exhibition projects are being presented across the city in collaboration with the City of Atlanta and university galleries, the art museum, and other visual arts institutions. As well, its performance programs are growing from street and open venues to major theater events. This expansion coincides with Atlanta's business and civic leaders' continued interest in energizing the downtown area, bringing greater cultural opportunities and building on city improvements that were given impetus by the Games. Atlanta itself has grown from its 1996 experiences. So, too, the Festival has benefited from our conversations as it lays out a bigger garden for the years ahead.

7
Two locally organized conversations followed in response to the summer series: Young Hughley brought together the hip-hop artists from the exhibition he had organized for the September 1996 Festival, "Sampling an Insistent Beat"; and Xenia Zed and myself organized a concluding conversation entitled "Conversations in the Post-Olympia" in an effort to reground these discussions back into the Atlanta arts community.

"**Conversation at The Castle**" was an unlikely event for Atlanta, for the Arts Festival, and for the time of the 1996 Centennial Olympic Games — or so it seemed. I had been invited by the Festival to do a "public art exhibition" that would involve commissioning new projects in the community and that could gain greater exposure for the organization at a uniquely visible moment in Atlanta, while also helping to define aspects of an artistic philosophy for the Festival as it moved into the future.

As with other large-scale programs I'd organized during this decade, the original prospectus presented to me became something to bounce off of; the following year and a half was a period of many changes as I and the Festival staff learned of each other's thoughts and needs, responded

MARY JANE JACOB staged the first retrospectives of American and European artists Magdalena Abakanowicz, Gordon Matta-Clark, and Jannis Kounellis, among the many exhibitions she organized during her tenures as chief curator at the Museum of Contemporary Art, Chicago, and MOCA, Los Angeles, in the 1980s. Exploring art outside the museum context, she has worked since 1990 as an independent curator organizing exhibitions that test the boundaries of public space and the relationship of contemporary art to audience. These have included "Places with a Past: New Site-Specific Art in Charleston" and "Culture in Action: New Public Art in Chicago" as well as "Conversations at The Castle." In Chicago, where she is based, she has also commissioned permanent public art projects by Ronald Jones and Louise Bourgeois. Jacob is consulting curator for The Fabric Workshop and Museum, Philadelphia, where she is organizing an international touring program, "Changing Spaces," for which she has commissioned experimental artists projects. She is also a Visiting Research Fellow under a Getty Residency at Bard College's Center for Curatorial Studies where she is on the graduate faculty. Jacob received a BFA from the University of Florida and an MA in history of art and museum studies from the University of Michigan.

to decreasing resources in the arts — trying to see them as new possibilities rather than limitations — and sought out a form by which to best communicate the ideas that emerged in the course of our conversations. During an extended period of development and through an organic process, my institutional partners and I, always in concert with the selected artists, found that from different starting points we came together and reinforced one another's ideas, making the program richer and more grounded.

The exhibition that resulted took place in a public space, but it was not public art — it was about public issues in art. The umbrella of the Festival proved not only to be the institutional support mechanism but also the framework for a discussion about the relationship of public and contemporary art. Such festivals are public par excellence. Atlanta's version draws more people in nine days than attend most art museums (including the local High Museum of Art) in several years' time. But festivals as venues for contemporary art are dismissed by the art world. Why such disdain when so many arts institutions are struggling to get larger and more diversified audiences? Their popular appeal, the mix of art, crafts, performances, food, and gaiety, seems to connote a lack of seriousness and quality. In the mass audience setting of a festival, the general assumption of contemporary art cognoscenti is that the art must be of the lowest common denominator.[1] Never mind that cafes, openings, members' parties, corporate and private space rentals, dancing, auctions, and other such activities take place in the art museum, at times forcing exhibition installations and public programming to change or be compromised. Thus, while the Festival was the initiator and organizing agent for this project, its own publicness was at the center of our inquiry: How can contemporary art and the broader, uninitiated, non-art-world public meet and to what end? Where do art experiences happen? What are the appropriate venues for contemporary art in the United States?

At one of the many fundraising visits I made over eighteen months, a foundation program officer said, "But how are you going to compete with the sound bites of the Olympics?" I replied, "We are not. We are going to have a conversation." With the many events — cultural and other — staged to celebrate, entertain, or just occupy a space on the occasion of the 1996 Olympics, we chose to compete in a different way, first engaging a relatively small number of Atlantans as collaborators and visitors — participants in a conversation — and then the larger contemporary art field, in each arena investigating: In American culture today, are contemporary art and the general public opponents or on the same side?

1
Linda Nochlin's study of the historic struggle over the democratization of art and of the museum as "a democratic instrument" concludes that: "What is revealed by an examination of the available material on the relation of the public to the museums from the nineteenth century to the present day is that the dimension of art works which sophisticated art historians, critics, avant-garde artists or enlightened musem workers consider 'esthetic' has generally been irrelevant, incomprehensible or antipathetic to the people as a whole." Linda Nochlin, "Museums and Radicals: A History of Emergencies," *Art in America* 59, 4 (July-August 1971): 37.
The notion that a large, mass audience is not possible or not desirable for contemporary art, or that to serve such an audience requires a lessening of quality, is indicated by Marcia Tucker's critique of museum practice: "Museums don't really want to respond to what audiences want, because we have such a low opinion of what they'll come up with. We aren't interested in democracy, because we think it would mean 'lowering our standards.'" Marcia Tucker, "The Art Museum Today: Who Is Its Audience?," unpublished notes for a panel discussion, The Metropolitan Museum of Art, New York, October 13, 1993.

Benjamin Buchloh posits that a new audience might be possible by changing the models for looking at art. He begins with evoking "a theory behind it, one that articulates that the traditional audience that we assume to be capable of receiving the multiplicity of aesthetic structures is a privileged audience. This argument says, We don't want to address this numinous 'universal' audience anymore. We want to address, with very clearly circumscribed statements, a different type of audience, one that is not privileged in the traditional sense of prepared reading competence. In order to reach out to that audience, in order to communicate at all, we have to make a sacrifice — a sacrifice in the range of aesthetic differentiations and subject constructions operative in the work." He then suggests that it might be worth considering if such an argument might be "able to produce a different type of audience in the museum, a different type of artist, a different type of communication and competence." As for artists, he offers, "Why can't one say, I define my project to be opening up venues, addressing new audiences, providing models of enactment, empowerment, articulation?" Finally, he states "there are other models to be constructed altogether, less obvious ones and perhaps more difficult ones, along the parameters of class. Difference can also be determined by other criteria, such as accessibility, communicability, particular targeting of audiences traditionally excluded from cultural access, whether in the institution or in production." Benjamin Buchloh, et al., "The Politics of the Signifier: A Conversation on the Whitney Biennial," *October* 66 (Fall 1993): 11–12, 14.

There are certain suppositions among arts and education professionals about the public as an audience for contemporary art that seem to be set up as hurdles. Maybe these assumptions are even barricades to defend the positions of some camps, lending to contemporary art an air of sophistication, intellectualization, and class that, it is said, can only be appreciated by a refined and restricted group. This position promotes an image of art's inaccessibility to the public and of its indifference to the concerns of everyday life. Who is contemporary art for?

In designing this program, I began from the position that the same work can speak to many different audiences simultaneously and that it can have multiple points of access that draw upon the many types of knowledge we learn over the course of our lives. With the artists, I organized the program around certain concepts: that contemporary art can matter, that it can move the beholder, relate to and be a useful and necessary part of many people's lives, irrespective of their social or economic circumstances; that it plays a role in the survival of culture and the human spirit even in the most devastating of situations; and that art is not a luxury just for those who have leisure time or can afford the acquisition of art objects. Most of all, we posited that art is not less important if it can be appreciated by a diverse or un-art-educated audience.

Proof of this position had been offered of late by new genre or community-based public art. But this art has its detractors who mistrust its alliance with the public (especially with so-called marginal sectors) and who oppose its aesthetics, or lack thereof, to their definition of art. The basic elements of the current critical debate around community-based art might be defined in three ways. First, the categorization dilemma: art or non-art? Does a work's social content of present-day issues or its ability to aid in bringing about community development or individual self-esteem diminish its importance as an artistic statement?[2] Second, the collaborative crisis. Traditionally, it has been felt that artists should maintain a distance from the masses in order to preserve the integrity of their artistic vision; in the case of public commissions, artists must have artistic authority. If we accept a social role for art, can community members have an involve-ment in the decision making? Can they participate in a process of using art as a means to bring about economic, political, social, or personal change? Lastly is the analysis of effectiveness. If we accept that art can have an effect on daily life, the question arises: To what end? Is it constructive enough, on enough people, and for long enough? Has the artist given enough of his or her time to the project? Are several months enough time for an artist to dedicate to a community project? A year? Several years?

To me, at this time in the discourse of international contemporary art exhibitions, it wasn't possible to do a community-based program, a public art program, a site-specific show, or a critique of history or cultural identity (though I had been involved in organizing these kinds of projects in the past). These formats were no longer sufficiently articulate to move the dialogue in the field of contemporary art, its institutions and audiences. Not because their proliferation had made them no longer novel; to a degree they are here to stay as ways in which we present the work of living artists. But rather because new questions had emerged out of the short, about ten-year, history of

important thing [curator Klaus Kertess] brings to the Whitney, since the last biennial, in 1993, was one of the museum's most embarrassing critical disasters ... it emphasized political art over all else and included considerably less painting than in previous shows, leaving critics to shriek that the Whitney had abandoned the very idea of art as a visual medium." Paul Goldberger, "The Art of His Choosing," *The New York Times Magazine*, February 26, 1995. A recent version of this sentiment can be found in Christopher Knight's review of "Uncommon Sense," an exhibition at the Museum of Contem-porary Art, Los Angeles, in 1996 that tried to bring the outside (community issues and community art) into the museum: "replacing a culture of complaint with a thera-peutic ideal reminds you that touting moral good-ness is beside art's point. Giving convincing visual form to ideas is what really counts." Christo-pher Knight, "The Socio-Art Genre," *Los Angeles Times*, March 18, 1997, F1, F9.

2
The inappropriateness of social and political agen-das in art has been widely held and loudly voiced by critics during this decade. Voluminous press argued this issue around the 1993 Whitney Biennial, summa-rized by the following remarks on the succeed-ing event: "This breadth of taste may be the most

such exhibitions. It was necessary instead to return to an ostensibly more traditional frame: a single location, a gallery space in which objects and installations are on view for anyone to visit. It was important to integrate aspects of new artistic and curatorial practice arising out of site or community and then link these ways of working to art conceived inside the artist's studio, and in doing so to demonstrate that both approaches can lead to an art that connects in actual and real ways with multiple audiences. It was important to ground the experience of art in the visual evidence of the work of art and then to expand the conversation with the audience. In this way I hoped we might address the division that had arisen in the field with the advent of site-specific and new public art, while considering the distance that has long existed between contemporary art and the popular audience.

I wanted to return to a reconsideration of the nature of the art experience as an emotional and intellectual engagement whose visual clues could be personally touching, socially or politically relevant, or spiritually moving irrespective of circumstances of time and place. I wanted to create a forum where the art and the artist could come directly in touch with the audience with as little intervention and interference as possible. The nurturing of a dialogue between artists and public seemed particularly urgent at this time when this relationship was cast as fearful or frivolous in the United States. It was necessary so that the contributions of the individual artist to society at large might be better understood. Could an exhibition be a mode of communication with the public, and in what ways could its form enhance the art experience?

By opening up avenues for artists to be in dialogue with segments of the public, I hoped to locate points of meaning in contemporary art for those outside the art world. I wanted to see if we could expand the audience for contemporary art by way of the artist's practice, that is, by bringing into the exhibition format those interactive, participatory, and generous aspects of contemporary artists' ways of working that are rooted in performance and community models. This necessitated not only inviting artists who could have a public presence — on view in the gallery during a performance or in open dialogue with community members during the development of their work — but also bringing the artists into the very thinking around the construction of the program. Undertaking the artistic and curatorial directions in tandem, the artists and I challenged each other as we shaped our ideas and designed our work through a continuous dialogue.

The notion of conversations proved to be a workable and inspirational concept for the artists — a gravitational point. This surpassed my own expectations since the idea of conversations had originally taken the form of a community speakers program, a major educational aspect of the overall program. As a theme for the artists' projects, conversation became a way of making art and was, at times, the work of art itself. Assuming a discursive mode enabled these projects to demonstrate some ways in which contemporary art can avoid being intimidating or irrelevant to the public. Unlike the classic museum-label dilemma centered around word count and academic grade level, and in defiance of the cardinal museum rule to simplify for the general public, the artists opened up complex ideas for dialogue, sometimes provocatively and speculatively. The conversations with the public that ensued were often multilayered, lengthy, and always surprising, leading in unplanned directions.

Public participation and investment took several forms: in the gallery as part of the artwork; in the community as a project was negotiated; through formal and informal gatherings throughout the summer; and over the Internet, reflecting the artists' keen interest in new technologies. All the works of art that resulted were built out of direct, personal involvement on the part of audience members. Studio-based artists Regina Frank and IRWIN were encouraged to foster a greater connection to visitors and then take their responses into consideration as they molded the subsequent phases and forms of their projects; unlike most art, their work was not static, complete at the time of opening, but dependent on and shaped by conversations. Community-based artists Ery Camara, Mauricio Dias and Walter Riedweg, and Maurice O'Connell were asked to develop modes of presentation that would bring their work in communities back into the exhibition space and allow for the experience of visitors in addition to those with whom they collaborated.

I felt it was important to challenge the essentialist argument that only those the project is about or made with can be its audience and to show that this art can be meaningful to multiple publics. Moreover, by including different genres, I hoped to elude the equation of one type of public with a particular type of art (namely, marginal communities with community-based art) and move beyond the chasms that had developed in the contemporary art field, voiced by critics and shared by some museum professionals and others in the art world since the 1980s focus on the community-specific agendas of multiculturalism, political interventionist art, and new public art. I wanted to show how art objects and community-based process share certain aspects and goals; how each deals with aesthetic issues and the issue of the larger culture at once; and how each is significant for our understanding of the dynamic between art and audiences in institutions. As Ery Camara put it, "In breaking down the museum walls and going to the community, we find new materials and new meanings that are needed to come back into the museum."

I thought it would be useful to enlarge this debate, which had reached a tense and confrontational point in the United States, around the idea of art or social work by featuring examples of community practice from other countries since such work was finding resonance in many places. Perhaps expanding the dialogue to an international level would offer some new ways of thinking about it. Viewed as a project during the Olympics, this direction also addressed a gap perceived in the cultural and community programming in Atlanta at the time, adding a significant international contemporary art component. This plan made connections as well to segments of the Atlanta population not directly touched by the Cultural Olympiad; even though "Conversations" involved relatively small numbers of people, it did so in substantial ways on a very personal level of exchange. Finally, this exhibition and public program lasted three months, unlike most of the Cultural Olympiad offerings, including temporary public artworks that were

19

Jacob

limited to one month around the Olympics. Thus, while the group of participating artists were from afar, our main audience was comprised of those who lived in Atlanta, either as collaborators in the projects or visitors to The Castle. Meanwhile, we saw this project as addressing ideological questions about art and audience, adding a critical edge to this moment of celebration that we hoped might in part help realize the Olympic dream of a "legacy" by having a lasting effect on the Festival's future programming and by contributing to the dialogue in the field around issues of international vs. local and the relationship of artists, institutions, and audience.

FROM PROPOSAL TO PROGRAM: "ATLANTA IN THE WORLD COMMUNITY"

I began by looking at the context of Atlanta during the Olympics, not to create a site-specific show but a meaningful one. Olympic events hold the promise of being a catalyst for change and progress within cities, along with garnering worldwide attention and glory. Like world's fairs of an earlier era, they become galvanizing forces for urban transformation. Left in the wake of rhetoric, known more through media than direct experience, local populations often find it hard to reconcile such hopes with reality. What would this "once in a lifetime" event mean in most people's lives? What would the populace of Atlanta learn of the world and the world of Atlanta?

As a new corporate mecca and fast-growing urban center, Atlanta had acquired the self-image of being an international city. But what does it mean to be international today? Atlanta is indeed a corporate center and world force of economic power. Does the meaning of international solely reside in the realm of commerce? What about the makeup of its population, which, distinct among southeastern cities, is now drawn from around the world? Or maybe its international identity is located in how Atlanta contributes to the well-being of the world, how it is affecting people's lives worldwide and contributing to the future. Could we highlight this role, that is, Atlanta as the world headquarters of CARE rather than Coca-Cola?

Art is a way of thinking about the world. We are not only connected by new technology or transnational events of vast proportions such as wars or ecological devastation but also by our shared humanity. So rather than emphasize the uniqueness of place in a geographic or cultural sense, I looked at focusing the exhibition on common needs and concerns as addressed by artists who continue an age-old tradition of grappling with questions of human existence through art. This exhibition would depart from the Olympics' focus as an international spectacle to address instead global social and cultural concerns. Audiences would be encouraged to think about the world through works of art, to recognize how culture is essential to the survival of every community, and to consider the role the artist serves in society.

Coming from different hemispheres, artists would be invited to make work as citizens of the world. Through their art, visitors would learn about social circumstances in their part of the world. Most of the work would have been made in the artists' studios, some assembled as installations on location, and a few developed out of artists' residencies in Atlanta communities.

Jacob

Alliances would be made, too, with locally based humanitarian organizations whose missions relate to the artists' own perspectives, paralleling their work in addressing the needs of humanity with the artists' subjects.[3]

    The proposed exhibition had to be in one location. (There were so many events and public artworks around the city that a scattered-site approach would defuse our efforts; anyway, normal routes of travel during the Olympics would be hampered.) The location had to be accessible and attractive — of compelling interest to visit in its own right. The meaning of the works on view would not be dependent on the physical description or historical associations of that place as in site-specific art. What was more important was that the place have a relationship to audience. It had to be a setting for coming together, a comfortable environment for conversation. But it could not be a museum or other established public gallery space whose identity would circumscribe its audience — a public space with privatizing connotations.

    The location we found was one of the few old buildings remaining in the city center, The Castle as it is affectionately called locally. Everyone knew it, but nobody had gone inside for years. It served as inspiration, exhibition space, and center for operations and activities; it was a meeting ground, a site of inquiry. The Castle's original use as a home was significant in that it posed a counterpoint to most public facilities in Atlanta today. Its intimate domestic interior made it a good place for sharing ideas, while also providing a psychic home for the participating artists from other countries.

3
These agencies include: The Carter Center and The Martin Luther King Center for Non-Violent Social Change; the world headquarters of CARE; the national headquarters of the Centers for Disease Control and Prevention; Southern Christian Leadership Conference; Habitat for Humanity; Boys & Girls Clubs; and The Friendship Force International; and regional or city offices of Amnesty International, UNICEF, Save the Children, The American Red Cross, World Relief, and the NAACP, among others.

Jacob

THE CASTLE

The Castle, a majestic and formidable five-story structure in midtown Atlanta, was built between 1909 and 1913 by Ferdinand Dallas McMillan. It is the sole reminder of the past in the midst of a corporate and cultural center now surrounded by the two AT&T regional towers (p. 23) and across from the Woodruff Arts Center, home to the Atlanta College of Art, High Museum of Art, and Alliance Theater. Although this building acquired its present appellation over the years due to its unusual appearance within the contemporary cityscape, McMillan, a former Confederate officer, dubbed his home "Fort Peace." Indeed its imposing medieval fortress-like exterior walls of granite from nearby Stone Mountain (the site of Mount Rushmore artist Gutzon Borglum's unfinished *Confederate Memorial*) are punctuated with slits and holes originally intended to be filled with flowers and bird nests in place of guns and cannons.

The structure's 11,000 square feet of interior space are enhanced by outdoor terraces and porches (p. 21). The two main stories of the house have essentially the same floor plan: four large rooms divided by a wide, grand hallway. Over the fireplaces of each room are the original plaster seals of the eight states in the Cotton States and International Exposition Centennial of 1895 (p. 25). The lower two levels, a carriage entrance and mezzanine, occupy the stone base of this building and are completely independent with no interior access to the house structure above. In these lower stories ship references are incorporated: ceiling trusses based on boat building techniques are on both floors and a rounded porch off the street side of the mezzanine resembles the deck of a ship (pp. 2-3). The ground level, or carriage entrance, is distinctive for its interior walls of unfaced granite blocks and grotto along the rear wall, originally to be the setting for a miniature scene of Hannibal crossing the Alps. Intended as an indoor swimming pool, the vast space of mezzanine was later used as a theater.

After The Castle was no longer a family residence, it functioned as a boarding house, restaurant, headquarters for the Atlanta Theatre Guild, and facility for other local arts and civic organizations. AT&T took possession of the building in 1987. For "Conversations at The Castle," the ground level was the site of installations by IRWIN and Regina Frank, who was followed by Ery Camara. The mezzanine level housed the installations of Mauricio Dias and Walter Riedweg; Maurice O'Connell's office of *Brothers for Others*; a public Internet center; staff offices (p. 14); and a large-scale meeting space (see front endpage) in which conversations were held, including several evenings in the "Conversations on Culture" series. Just outside the entrance to this level, steps led up to the deck by Yukinori Yanagi and down to the ramp to street level.

Our original plan was to use the entire house with each artist occupying one of the rooms of the upper-story living quarters with a work, installation, or performance. This facility also inspired the concept of "conversations" as a speakers' program, not an adjunct but an integral component of equal stature and significance to the exhibition itself.

Who can speak for art? Who is authorized to communicate their experience of art to others? Guides, informants, witnesses, scholars, practitioners, viewers; I imagined a hundred or more Atlantans of different backgrounds and walks of life each finding their room at The Castle, the work of art that touched them most, relating their perceptions about this work and engaging their neighbors and visitors from around the world in informal, on-the-spot discussions. They would speak less from the vantage point of art history than from knowledge and understanding gained from their own personal experiences, their particular cultures or vocations. They would activate the exhibition through dialogue, connecting art to life — their lives — and from there to the lives of others. At least one speaker would be on site at all times, but sometimes simultaneous conversations would be going on in different rooms. They could be brief or extended; the visitor could join in or eavesdrop, as we do with conversations. The conversations would be as varied as the lives of the individuals themselves.

Through participation and sharing, the "Conversations Program" would multiply the meaning of the art and offer the possibility of extending the traditional museum-going audience to other realms of the general public. Here the untrained, non-art-academic experience — often deemed less valid by the museum — would form the core. Enlightenment, education, enjoyment can be found through what one brings to the viewing of a work of art and not just in what one is instructed to get out of the work; in fact, the latter can be in direct opposition to a reaction based on personal or cultural knowledge. We believed that personal experience could provide an important entry to art.

But the cost to use the entire building proved prohibitive because of the building's inherent, much deteriorated condition and its lack of handicap accessibility, requiring significant exterior construction of temporary structures for access and egress. With increased attention to city codes precipitated by the oncoming Olympics, other security and fire protection measures, including a sprinkler system throughout, were among the required modifications.

So a radical shift was proposed. The lower two floors could be most readily and economically made usable. They were the structural foundation of the house; they could be the place from where we would build a foundation for larger ideas. I would invite a smaller number of artists but for a longer stay, a summer residency; they would ground the project and focus on the most pressing concerns about contemporary art and its audience that had motivated us thus far. If the number of artists and works had to be reduced, then, to me, the artists most essential to represent were those whose projects could be publically interactive. And instead of an educational program based on relaying personal interpretations, conversations took on another form — metaphoric and actual — through participation routes that the artists would develop with the

audience they directly brought into or engaged with their project.

There were still significant renovations to be made: most prominently, removing the theater stage and old bathroom/dressing rooms; creating a raised ceiling, in effect an elevated room between floors, for the IRWIN hanging (p. 72); and installing functional plumbing and electricity, as there was none. One of the most challenging needs was to provide a means of handicap access between the two floors. The cost of an elevator was prohibitive, so Merrill Elam of Scogin Elam & Bray, based in Atlanta, designed an exterior ramp along the side of the house. In order for a wheelchair to negotiate the steep grade, it had to switch back and forth four times. This would be a major physical and visual presence. So the question arose: how to make this architectural element express what we wanted to say with the program?

Early in 1995, Homi Bhabha and I began discussing the ideas around this project during our regular conversations since he had moved to Chicago. In spring 1996 we conducted a series of interviews in Atlanta with civic, corporate, and cultural leaders about their takes on culture, cultural events, the Olympics, internationalism, global community, and diversity. Out of these conversations the same words kept coming up, though used in different ways. Bhabha linked these words and we put them on the sides of the ramp (see cover, p. 23). Common words, they took on multiple meanings in their placement and combination row by row and across sections of ramp. They formed a curious and thought-provoking type of signage, unlike the consumer-directed graphics that filled the streets of Atlanta—and every-

Jacob

where else—during the Olympics. These words stood as symbols of the ideas we were grappling with in the overall project.

To complement the interior space, where access was now limited to half the house, and to open up the building and be more hospitable, a deck — a kind of patio — was created at the top of the ramp, covering over an unused area adjacent to the AT&T corporate tower's service areas. This location became the site of Yukinori Yanagi's ¿Tierra Nuestra? (pp. 26, 108–9) and a gathering point for many planned and unplanned conversations.

TALKING WITH THE AUDIENCE: "CONVERSATIONS AT THE CASTLE"

With a shared interest in the role of art as a communication vehicle, the artists in "Conversations at The Castle" created projects that took the form of public interaction. Art, to them, was a mode of conversation. The artists' presence, whether at The Castle or in communities and then later at the exhibition site, added a human dimension to their work that made it real and more compelling. Here the art experience, even though in a public setting, was one that touched audience members on an intensely personal level.

The artists worked in several different ways and their projects were presented in stages. In June, during the first phase, Regina Frank inhabited her installation for seven weeks. The IRWIN installation shared the same gallery; there the artists staged an opening night performance, replacing their bodies with clothed and painted plaster casts while they traveled across the United States by recreational vehicle, staging conversations that were transmitted back to this location via the Internet. At the same time, on the mezzanine above as well as in different places around Atlanta where the other artists were working, discussions between artists and others outside the art world took place daily.

Yukinori Yanagi – ¿Tierra Nuestra?

The United Nations emblem provides the basis for the image of Yukinori Yanagi's massive floor painting ¿Tierra Nuestra?, installed on the deck between the AT&T tower and The Castle. This "symbol of all nations" was created more than half a century ago at a time when the Western/Northern hemispheres dominated the world, reapportioned it, and drew up new national boundaries. Yanagi's design inverts the perspective, employing a point of view from south of the equator. With this work the artist critiques the privileged position implied in this global symbol, which represents various parts of the word unequally, while his title asks the question "Our World?" in Spanish (spoken by nearly 300 million people), asserting the position of those peoples considered to be marginal. ¿Tierra Nuestra? was originally created by Yanagi in 1994 as a flag; here it became a backdrop and conversation point for many gatherings, both planned and spontaneous.

Yukinori Yanagi was born in Fukuoka, Japan in 1959. He graduated from Musashino Art University in Tokyo with a BFA in 1983 and an MFA in 1985. In 1988 he became a post-graduate fellow at Yale University, receiving an MFA in sculpture there in 1990. His work The World Flag Ant Farm catapulted him to international attention when he won a young artist's award at the 1993 Venice Biennale. In this work national identities were lost as the flags of all 170 United Nations member nations, made from boxes of colored sand, were dissolved by migrating harvester ants, pointing to the interdependence of nations through trade and immigration. Another ant farm work, Atlantic, based on the ninety-seven flags of countries bordering the Atlantic Ocean, was included in the 1996 Cultural Olympiad in Atlanta.

Jacob

In August, Ery Camara's installation based on his residency during June and July in Reynoldstown replaced Regina Frank's (she moved the physical location of her piece to Tokyo, remaining tied to The Castle via the Internet). The IRWIN installation remained, but the artists returned to Slovenia with their Russian colleagues and began to incorporate reports from their American travels into European exhibition contexts. Mauricio Dias and Walter Riedweg had completed their workshops at a youth detention center and federal penitentiary; they created two installations at The Castle that were public manifestations of their experiences aimed to further community conversations. Also during this phase, after having spent months at a Boys & Girls Club and its parent organization's executive offices, Maurice O'Connell took up residence at The Castle. Unlike Frank's public presence — a performance behind glass, communicating through electronic and silent gestures — O'Connell's practice was art vérité, exceedingly vocal and verbal as visitors came to his actual, albeit temporary, office for extended times to debate questions of youth and society.

Finally, in late August, artway of thinking — the Venetian collaborative of Federica Thiene and Stefania Mantovani — orchestrated *Chow*, which gave life to the symposium series "Conversations on Culture." This final coming together of the artists, staff, and many others who had been involved in the project with art professionals from elsewhere was a chance to discuss the ideas that affected each of the participants in their own work, ideas that were embodied in the artists' projects. For this series of dinner discussions, I asked Michael Brenson to join me in inviting the guests and session leaders and in shaping the topics.[4] In 1996–97, he worked as editor of the "Conversation on Culture" section of essays written by the authors in the months just following our discussions.

The projects comprising "Conversations at The Castle" cannot be summarized by a single theme but cross multiple themes that, when taken together, give a richness and depth to the whole program. The Olympics was an unmistakable backdrop. All the artists considered how the concept of international is constructed in the art world and through global events such as the Olympics. Sports as the focus of the moment in Atlanta had metaphorical implications for some of them. O'Connell used as his starting point a 1948 French document *"La regle du jeu"* ("The Rules of The Game"), which outlines how one should participate in society. It became a historical precedent for the sports metaphor that O'Connell relocated in the Boys & Girls Clubs' use of sports as a means of developing the individual. This subject also led to a greater exploration of the complex social relationships that permit a child to be a player in life. Both Regina Frank and IRWIN undertook a kind of marathon: Frank traveling from Berlin to Atlanta, stopping en route in Venice for beads and in a Japanese village to make the kimono; IRWIN traveling across country.

Another element that runs through several works was youth — the hailed but often token or forgotten beneficiary of the Olympics.[5] Developing strategies outside traditional routes of art

4

Other informal sessions completing the offerings for this two-week period included: "New Curatorial Roles" led by Anna Harding, Course Director, Visual Arts Department, Goldsmith's College, London; "Changing Critical Approaches" led by Jeffrey Kastner, Associate Editor, *ARTNews*, New York; "Youth, Art and Crime" led by Bill Cleveland, Director of Education, Walker Art Center, Minneapolis; and "New Parameters of Public Art" led by Jennifer MacGregor-Cutting, art advisor, Hartford.

5

Before the Olympics we were told: "The program created by Congress to develop America's Olympic athletes is failing.... The USOC's [United States Olympic Committee's] mission includes responsibility to build the next generation of Olympic athletes. But, since 1989, its direct grants for community sports have totaled barely more than $1 million — one-fifth of 1 percent of its $544 million in revenues for that period." Joe Drape, "The 'Shocking' Truth — Very Little Olympic Cash Goes to Development," *The Atlanta Journal-Constitution*, October 1, 1995. Drape goes on to point out that direct mail and fund-raising pitches "boast of combatting violence and drug abuse. They say donations help develop kids through such organizations at the Boys and Girls Clubs of America and the Amateur Athletic Union (AAU).... But if contributors think that money is finding its way to the streets and playgrounds of America, they are wrong." Joe Drape, "U.S. Olympic Committee makes misleading sales pitch to America," *The Atlanta Journal-Constitution*, October 1, 1995.

education, Camara, Dias and Riedweg, and O'Connell all embraced this audience. Camara, an artist and museum professional, challenged institutional museum education through his workshop discussions and in his installation, which analyzed the politics of museum display. Dias and Riedweg combined their techniques and experience as teachers with their practice as artists. O'Connell questioned the motivations and benefits of the visible corporate-initiated Olympic youth programs, while asking others to speak with him about the ongoing work of not-for-profit social agencies devoted to youth.

For all the artists, conversation across and within cultures began with the personal (speaking directly to other individuals), moved to the more public visitor level, and arrived at the technological (the Internet) as a way of extending the conversations beyond Atlanta in place and time. And while installations were the visible result, it was the artists' research into thinking about the experience of art by the audience that is perhaps the most valuable contribution of this program. For the Festival and myself, it was important not only to offer each artist an occasion to make a new and ambitious work — for most of them it was their first opportunity to show in the United States — but also to provide them with the physical and mental space to explore and share ideas and move the thinking in the field.

For this publication I asked the artists to reflect on the process of development of their projects and their encounters and engagement with audience. This request initiated a several-month, post-event conversation that has resulted in the writings contained in the artists section that follows. It was important that this occur after the fact; theirs were not projects that in any way could have been represented or fully considered in a catalogue at the time of the exhibition. Rather we took the months that followed, as did Michael Brenson with other authors in this book, to continue a conversation started in Atlanta. The success of our work will be measured in the new conversations it precipitates.

29

Jacob

INTRODUCTION TO
"CONVERSATIONS ON CULTURE"
Michael Brenson

The conversations over dinner, or in one instance over lunch, that formed the final part of the "Conversations at The Castle" program grew out of an awareness that many people who care deeply about art and culture need to be able to struggle openly and collectively with the extraordinary questions that define this moment — questions like: What does art mean? What is an artist? Who is art for? What makes the experience of art possible?

While there are many interrelated reasons why this is more a moment of questions than of answers, any attempt to understand the widespread uncertainty in the art and culture communities must consider the crisis of the National Endowment for the Arts — the cultural issue, more than any other, that has defined this decade in the United States. It is not just that the endow-

MICHAEL BRENSON is an independent critic, curator, and educator. After receiving a PhD in art history from Johns Hopkins University, he moved to Paris where he remained for nine years, writing for *Art in America* and the *International Herald Tribune*. He returned in 1982 to join the staff of *The New York Times*. Since leaving the *The Times* in 1991, he has worked extensively on modern and contemporary sculpture, writing on Magdalena Abakanowicz, Elizabeth Catlett, Mel Edwards, Alberto Giacometti, Luis Jimenez, Richard Serra, Joel Shapiro, David Smith, Tony Smith, and Ursula von Rydingsvard; and curating "Magdalena Abakanowicz: War Games" at New York's P.S. 1 Museum and "Ryoji Koie: The Energy of Fire" at New York's Gallery at Takashimaya. With his essay "Healing in Time" for *Culture in Action* (Bay Press, 1994) he began a meditation on the meanings and possibilities of the sculptural experience when the focus is not on an object but rather a participatory interaction between artist and audience that unfolds in space and time. He has lectured widely on public art and on the effects of the National Endowment for the Arts crisis. He has been a consultant for the Rockefeller Foundation; is on the editorial board of *Art Journal*; and was a visiting critic at Yale University, the University of Texas, and Bard College's Center for Curatorial Studies.

ment crisis has raised many of the same issues that were brought to the surface by multicultural-ism, race, class, gender studies, and changing demographics, but rather that it raised them in a way that spotlighted the vulnerability of art and artists, as well as the insularity of the institution-alized art world whose job it is, in part, to fight for art and artists and demonstrate to the Ameri-can people why they matter.

This crisis has made it clear that if art is ever going to have a chance to be securely grounded in this country, the breach must be healed between contemporary art and those segments of the American population that have believed for some time that art and its institutions are indifferent to or negations of them and their values. People who have felt estranged in museums either because of the formality of the architecture, the institutional infatuation with social and economic power, or the absence of information about art to which they are eager to respond need to be able to visit museums without feeling belittled or intimidated. Communities with conventional religious and political beliefs who have been demonized by many artists since Impressionism have to be engaged by artists, curators, and other thinkers. Immigrants from Asia, Latin America, the Caribbean, and Eastern Europe, who may be rooted in very different artistic traditions than earlier immigrants from Western Europe, have to be welcomed into the largest artistic debates. The artistic imagination has to be exposed to young people in a way that inspires them to engage their environments and expand their knowledge of themselves.

If there is a word that defines the challenges and difficulties of the moment, it is audience. Audience is now a buzzword in many museums that are trying, through outreach programs, wall labels, interactive technology, and other means, to appeal to people who have not felt welcome in them. Audience is now also a buzzword in foundations, whose influence has increased as the National Endowment's funding has been cut back; many will only give money if increasing responsiveness to diverse audiences is built into the exhibition program. Indeed, there is so much pressure on museums to think about audience that the audience issue may be pitted against curatorial imagination. "Funding for exhibitions has diminished even as funding for audience analysis, marketing, and outreach programs has increased," notes Jacquelynn Baas. "We have come to use audience as a means of validating cultural activities and measuring their 'success,'" Susan Krane writes.

Just because museums develop audience analysis, marketing, and outreach programs does not mean that the audience issue is understood and dealt with. What does audience mean? Who is and who is not audience? Does the word encourage a connection with those different from us or just reinforce the kind of us versus them thinking that funding for audience analysis and development seems intended to break down? What is the nature of the relationship between institution (including trustees, patrons, and collectors) and audience when the site is a museum, where the art that focuses the exchange is owned by the institution, and visitors remain "visitors" no matter how satisfying the interaction may be between the audience and the museum staff? Does the funding pressure that has led many museums to allow certain audience concerns —

such as attendance and easy accessibility — to shape curatorial programming end up reinforcing the embittering conviction among some directors and curators that audience and aesthetic concerns are inherently in conflict?

At what point, the writer Nicholas Drake asked during one of the conversations in Atlanta, does appeal to audience become pandering? When does "our focus on audience confuse the issue and lead us to mistake 'market' for community, consumption for perception?" Krane asks. After decades of grave suspicion about the masses in many of the most influential modernist and postmodern circles, often understandably, how did we reach the point where the masses are now institutionally idealized?

How does the idea of audience, and with it the audience issue, become real to the point where we can understand its potential for human and aesthetic illumination and transformation? If, as Lisa Corrin writes, an audience is going to be understood and treated as "a complex and multifaceted group of individuals willing to engage the museum on equal terms," it is essential to consider how artists negotiate issues of ownership and power with those communities that are now being redefined by art museums as audience. To the degree that a frame exists in artist-community projects, the community largely defines it. When artists Ery Camara, Maurice O'Connell, Mauricio Dias, and Walter Riedweg work in communities in Atlanta, far removed from the institutional art world, audiences cease to be "audiences" and become complex and multifaceted individuals.

"Community-based endeavors like 'Conversations at The Castle,'" writes Krane, "are laboratories of practice — both social and artistic." They "frequently involve groups of people who do not traditionally attend museums…. They focus on process more than product, on the value of multiple voices, and on the irresolution and indeterminacy that exist in everyday life outside of institutional constructs." At The Castle, Krane says, "art is a vehicle for individualized, embodied communication. Personal circumstances, class, identity, and ethnicity stay in the foreground."

The relationships between artist and audience, and institution and audience, are debated throughout the essays in "Conversations on Culture." For the authors who have been strongly supportive of community-based art or the place of the community in the institution, there is a profound awareness of the human realities engaged by the artist or the institution and the need for the artist or curator to function first of all as an aware and responsible human being. Steven Durland underlines the distinction Maurice O'Connell makes between working "among" rather than "with or for the community." He also makes the crucial point that "for the community-based artist the ability to handle social negotiations and to treat cultural imperatives with sensitivity are not just personality traits but artistic skills necessary to realize an artwork." In her discussion with Tricia Ward about art and youth, Amina Dickerson reveals a deep sense of commitment to the young people she worked with at the Chicago Historical Society during a five-month museum mentoring program targeted to young African-American girls "at risk." Dickerson believed that the suddenness with which the program ended "let the girls down."

33

Brenson

As a result, she "resolved that as much as possible [she] would seek to create projects of longer duration, informed by [her] sense that projects in and of themselves are not enough."

This commitment and self-questioning, this sensitivity to others that must exist if audiences are going to be truly respected and engaged, are no less important to Ward, who, as an artist, has been working for several years with teenagers in Los Angeles to create and maintain a community youth art park. She feels equity is not only desirable in this park but also possible. It depends, she writes, upon creating a place of inclusiveness where people will not feel judged. It also depends upon longevity, that is to say, on her willingness to make this involvement part of her everyday life for an indefinite period. And it depends upon conversation, which ensures the necessary "level of communication." For Ward, securing her place in society depends upon her respect for and commitment to the people with whom she works. This respect and commitment require blurring "the boundaries between audience and artist, artist and community, [which] translates to artist as citizen."

What would it mean for museum curators to function first of all as citizens? In museums, is blurring the boundaries between institution and audience, curator and audience, possible — or desirable? What effect does the work of art have on this boundary? If museums believe, as I do, in the greatness of particular objects and their ability to function in personally and culturally life-affirming ways, how does this belief shape their relationships with their audiences? And if they set limits on that relationship, how can museums ensure that the revelatory power of paintings, sculptures, and photographs is constantly open to discovery and investigation, rather than simply being defined by the work of art's placement on a wall or floor as an emblem, or trophy, of institutional power?

Susan Vogel believes that in some museum presentations, equality, or even peaceful coexistence, among different cultures and viewpoints is impossible. For a curator who has to display a ceremonial object from one culture within the space of another culture that exploited and stigmatized it, or who has to conceive an installation that will be interpreted and experienced by very different audiences than those for which the work was made, conflict may be bitter and unresolvable. What she calls for is not caution and fear of controversy but the courage and will to take chances and accept and learn from discord and failure.

All the contributors to the "Conversations on Culture" section are aware of the challenges the audience issue poses for museums. Krane, like Vogel, has had to be responsive to the many interests represented within her museum. She asks how the various "systems of power, support and influence align themselves today" and how each one "circumscribes audience." Baas, who wants museums to become "labs of cultural understanding" in which "people can let their customary defenses down and learn to empathize with those who may be quite different from themselves," is conscious of the precarious balance between reaching out to audiences and using them. She believes that the recent commercial thinking that has led to the growth of bookstores, restaurants, and space rentals for weddings and bar mitzvahs in many museums offers new possi-

34

Brenson

bilities for appealing to a broader public and "engaging the whole person," but it also brings with it the potential for new forms of exploitation. For Baas, the new marketing methods and commercial possibilities must be thought about as seriously and as imaginatively as exhibitions.

Corrin, who has worked between museums and communities that have not been part of art museum audiences, believes that a full response to the challenges raised by the audience issue means changing the way museums operate and think. She imagines a museum within a museum that is conceived in part in order to "embrace the necessity of and implicit tension in engaging contemporary culture." This new institution, which she calls the contemporaneous museum, would present itself "as a laboratory and site of debate, where the language of visual culture and its institutions is part of an ongoing evolution in terms." In the era we are entering, Corrin believes "access to contemporary art and ideas will mean a commitment by museums to provide a context for the audience that creates conversation instead of a lecture." For her, meeting the audience challenge goes hand in hand with expanding and deepening the understanding of art and with the collective creation of culture.

"Conversations on Culture" was intended to be a laboratory and site of debate in which people within and outside institutions could engage one another first of all as citizens — that is to say, as people urgently concerned with communicating with one another with curiosity, openness, responsibility, and risk. The participants were not invited because they were influential, but because their experiences had led them to question how they work within the cultural field today. Each conversation included individuals able to trust their doubts and uncertainties and eager to transform them into meaningful art and culture. As they met for conversation over dinner, with no assigned seating arrangement and no distinction among the places at the table, there was no hierarchical distinction presumed between these artists, museum directors and curators, critics, community leaders from Atlanta, and other participants. They were able to communicate as equals and get a clearer sense of how many people who now want to make a difference share their need for what Krane calls "embodied communication."

The conversations were intended to encourage exploration of the place and meanings of art in the United States. But the titles of the program ("Conversations at The Castle") and of the discussions ("Conversations on Culture"), as well as the informality and open-endedness of the discussions, built into each conversation an awareness of the meanings and complexities of conversation itself — which will remain a buzzword as long as audience remains an urgent and inescapable issue — and a conviction that the process of conversing can have a texture and vitality that makes its connective tissue as important in the end as any idea expressed or any problem resolved within the conversation.

The authors who contributed to the "Conversations on Culture" section were designated as session leaders. They initiated the conversations but did not control them, participating on equal terms with all who attended. They were asked to write an essay following the event that would be long enough to make a statement but shorter than an academic treatise. They were encouraged

35

to write personally, colloquially — "conversationally" — so that their words could engage a range of interested readers. Their experiences of these evenings were fresh in their minds when they began writing, but they were not obliged to record what took place during the four-, five-, or six-hour conversations. Dickerson and Ward chose to approach their essay on "Youth, Art, and Society" as a continuing conversation between themselves.

The artists who worked in Atlanta communities all summer — Camara, O'Connell, Dias, and Riedweg — helped set the tone for the evenings. Even prior to "Conversations on Culture," they, along with Regina Frank and IRWIN, participated in weekly conversations with one another, the staff of "Conversations at The Castle," and others from Atlanta about the development of their work and the issues considered in this book. They brought to the conversations not only a belief in the artist as citizen but also respect for the realities of the people with whom they worked in Atlanta, as well as an ability to communicate to the other participants their commitments to young people in the poor and sometimes dangerous neighborhoods in which the youth live.

They also brought to the discussions the passion of their concerns with ownership and democracy. "Communication, not representation," Dias said. He spoke of the need for people to make themselves vulnerable and to "exchange territories," and of the importance of art that "takes away the frame rather than giving it." Riedweg stressed the importance of conflict in the creation of culture and the responsibility he felt to challenge the assumed meaning of every term. Camara brought to the conversations an awareness of his native Senegal and the assumptions Westerners have brought to their analyses and documentations of African cultures, as well as his resistance to polarities between private and public, national and international, audience and institution ("We are all audience and we are all institution," he said the first night). All of O'Connell's responses were marked by a radical unpretentiousness and by a conviction — in the shadow of the overpowering media circus of the Olympics, which had just ended — that "non-events" can generate as much meaning as spectacles.

The two artists most integral to "Conversations on Culture" were Federica Thiene and Stefania Mantovani (artway of thinking). Because of their involvement in preparing and designing all aspects of the meals, including serving the food, they were not consistently engaged in the discussions. At some point, usually just before dessert, they introduced themselves and Massimo Frigatti, the chef who had come with them from Venice, and they spoke for a few minutes about themselves, their culture, their rationale for the menu, and their holistic approach to art.

The conversations were remarkably intense. While they had topics, and while each had a place within the overall structure of the program, they were very loosely framed so as to allow the participants the greatest possible freedom in deciding where the conversation would go. Those of us who were present for all of the conversations that summer knew that it would take a long time to digest what had happened and unpack all the ideas and feelings compressed within them. The ideas and feelings expressed in this book coalesced over months of continuing communication. The essays in this section were conceived as an essential part of the process set in motion by the Atlanta conversations.

Editing, for me, meant continuing the conversations. Editor and author challenged and drew each other out, just as the participants in the group conversations challenged and drew each other out about the subjects raised. While reflecting on the texts, I felt as if I were in a room with the authors, responding to their thoughts with my own. Their ideas mattered to me, and I was convinced they were of genuine concern to anyone else wanting to make sense of this cultural moment. I was as open and direct and sometimes as incautious and opinionated as I am with friends. I made carefully considered comments and suggestions, but I also expressed strongly felt ideas and feelings that I knew they could use, reject, or define themselves against.

Now, writing this introduction, at the end of this project, after participating in all the conversations in Atlanta and communicating with these writers through much of the last year, several issues seem to me particularly worth emphasizing. At the beginning of her essay, Baas articulates three essential questions about art institutions: "First, who should our audience be," she asks, "everybody or only everybody who happens to be interested in art? Second, with our current state of diminished public funding, how can art institutions attract and keep new audiences? And finally, the big question: what is the purpose of art museums now?" These questions make me ask, what, indeed, is an art museum? With all the interests on which it depends, how much can it question itself? Does it have enough independence to continually ask itself, like the artists in Atlanta, like most thoughtful and introspective artists — why do we act as we do and do what we do? What does art mean to us? Who owns us? What is the place of art in society? What is our relationship with the American people?

Why have the defining words of the 1990s been so polarizing? Where did the words audience, public, and community come from? Who uses them and who doesn't? How does a word become a buzzword? Can we advocate words that are not polarizing, that allow for a discussion in which we are all audience, public, and community, so that the differences and similarities among us can be more clearly defined and debated? Is conversation this kind of word?

Finally, I believe in conversation. In the best conversations, no one is used; ownership is shared. Everyone leaves with a sense that the ideas exchanged belong to each person present. Everyone also leaves respecting those who were part of the exchange, whether or not there was agreement. For me, conversation does make connections, it helps make connection possible. In the most sustaining conversations, everyone is, at once, giver and receiver, producer and consumer, artist and audience. Just as important, in conversation being and becoming merge. The moment is complete in itself, but it always points toward the future even as it evokes the histories and struggles from which each feeling and idea emerged. Conversation, like art, gives access to the space of time.

37

Brenson

CONVERSATIONAL ART

Homi K. Bhabha

One way of thinking of wisdom, as something of which the love is not the same as
that of argument, and of which the achievement does not consist in finding the
correct vocabulary for representing essence, is to think of it as the practical wisdom
necessary to participate in a conversation.

— Richard Rorty, *Philosophy and the Mirror of Nature*

THE RESONANCE OF CONVERSATION

Conversation, as a curatorial idea, could be seen as an antidote to the connoisseurial "silence"
that traditionally accompanies the awesome presence of Art. It is, of course, a silence that is
surrounded by the cacophony of the auction room, the sagacity of the seminar, even the snobbery
of the salon: "In the room the women come and go/Talking of Michelangelo" as T. S. Eliot once
remarked. The art object may be labeled, contextualized, compared with catalogues, and
burdened by interpretation, but there remains a common assumption that a pervasive silence is
appropriate for aesthetic attention. It is a silence embedded in the very moment at which artistic
practice achieves its "objecthood," whether this happens in the atelier or the museum. In "Art and
Objecthood," Michael Fried deftly turns this moment of silence into the space of spectatorship
itself, where silence stands for a certain determining distance between the viewer and the viewed:
"The experience of being distanced from the work in question seems crucial: the beholder knows
himself to stand in an indeterminate, open-ended — and unexacting — relation as subject — to
the impassive object on the wall or on the floor. In fact, being distanced by such objects is not, I
suggest, entirely unlike being distanced or crowded by the *silent presence of another person*" (my
emphasis).[1] Although one might question Fried's wider "high modernist" agenda, he is surely right
when he suggests that the distance that separates subject and object also becomes the space in
which a certain ideological and institutional notion of "audience" comes to be constituted. I am,
of course, using audience in a double sense: to suggest both the encounter between the body of
the work and the public that stands before it — reception or consumption — as well as the defer-
ential attitude with which people often approach the temple of art — academy, museum, institute
— to seek an "audience" with some august, transcendent reality.

    Mary Jane Jacob's introductory essay — as well as the testimony of the participating artists —
makes it clear that the profound purpose in staging "Conversations at The Castle" was to shrink
this distance and shatter the silence. However, what is done in and through the practice of art

[1]
Michael Fried, "Art and
Objecthood," in *Art in
Theory 1900–1990: An
Anthology of Changing
Ideas,* ed. Charles Harri-
son and Paul Wood
(Oxford and Cambridge:
Blackwell, 1992), 826.

HOMI K. BHABHA was
born into the Parsi community of
Bombay, India. He received a BA
from Bombay University and an
MA and PhD from Christ Church,
Oxford University. Bhabha has
been a reader in English literature
at Sussex University; a senior
fellow and Old Dominion Visiting
Professor at Princeton University; the Steinberg Visiting
Professor at the University of
Pennsylvania, where he delivered
the Richard Wright Lecture
Series; and a faculty fellow in the
School of Criticism and Theory,
Dartmouth College. He is
currently the Chester D. Tripp
Professor in the Humanities at
the University of Chicago and
visiting professor of the humanities at University College,
London. Bhabha will be delivering
the W. E. B. Du Bois Lectures at
Harvard University and will be
Beckman Professor of English at
the University of California,
Berkeley, in 1999. He edited the
collection of essays *Nation and
Narration* (Routledge, 1990) and is
the author of *The Location of
Culture* (Routledge, 1994). He is
currently working on the book *A
Measure of Dwelling*, a history of
cosmopolitanism. Bhabha also
writes regularly for *Artforum*.

also requires acknowledgement in the language of criticism. What animates "Conversations," as a collaborative pursuit, is driven by the idea that the "distance that has long existed between contemporary art and the popular audience" — notice the return of Fried's point — can be overcome by a radical shift in the guiding curatorial metaphor, from the language of theatricality and display — exhibition, show, opening — to the ongoing evolution of the discursive experience — dialogue, conversation: in Jacob's words, a "forum where the art and the artist could come directly in touch with the audience with as little intervention and interference as possible. . . . [I]n defiance of the cardinal museum rule to simplify for the general public, the artists opened up complex ideas for dialogue, sometimes provocatively and speculatively. The conversations with the public that ensued were often multilayered, lengthy, and always surprising, leading in unplanned directions."

There can be no shortcut to the democratization of artistic production or circulation. Populist, agitprop approaches arrogantly assume that the "people" or the "masses" will follow. Nor can we be sanguine that the instant connectivity and accessibility of the new digital technologies will necessarily democratize artistic practices and communities. This new technological utopianism is as unconvincing as the influential "free market" myth that assumes that economic opportunity is equally open to all who trade in goods and services and effect rational choices. Pulling down the bastions of privilege or the edifices of elitism has never, in itself, assured a more democratic future. Democracy depends, to a great degree, on a culture of public belief that takes seriously the proposition that questions of value and knowledge are as deeply linked to the matter of cultural practice and public policy as the issues of morality and action are wedded to the concept of "good" citizenship.

It is in this cause that "conversational" art practice, to coin a phrase, speaks most profoundly and productively. It must be acknowledged that what intervenes and interferes, in a productive way, between the artists' intentions and the audience's expectations — museum committees, curators, and trustees notwithstanding — is the compulsion of the artwork itself to be a creative site of "unplanned directions" and "multilayered interpretations." Conversational art, dedicated to constructing its "object" and its "audience" through a process of ongoing dialogue, is committed to exploring contextual contingency in defining the nature and values of the aesthetic experience. It embodies an experience that cannot appropriately be defined within the current art-historical discussion, where the values of "painting" — the sign of a fast diminishing respect for the artist as auteur — are polemically pitted against public art projects that are considered to be the manufactures of a regnant *ressentiment*, or multiculturalism as it is so often called.

When "conversation" as a curatorial and creative process seeks to transform the distance between art and its audience, it does so by changing our sense of the "space" of the artwork itself, by making us rethink fundamental questions concerned with the category of the aesthetic. These questions are somehow prior to the critic's concern with genres and periods as the historical measure of art's social vision. The conversational approach poses these questions: What kind of "knowledge" do we expect from the practice and the presentation of art? How does conversation change our relation, as artists and audiences, to cultural experience and the social transformations of our times?

The term "conversation," as a way of understanding the dialogue between culture and community, has a rich philosophical genealogy that is crucial, in my view, to the aims of this project. My own phrase, contextual contingency, which I shall elaborate below as a way of reading the general vision of the show — multilayered dialogues, unplanned directions — as well as the strategies of individual works, owes much to the pioneering work of America's preeminent "liberal" pragmatist philosopher, Richard Rorty. In *Philosophy and the Mirror of Nature* (1979), a book that set the terms of philosophical discussion for a decade, he elaborates an "anti-epistemological" position, seeking to unsettle "the way in which the West became obsessed with the notion of our primary relation to objects as analogous to visual perception, and thus to suggest that there could be other conceptions of our relation to things."[2] What accompanies this "visualization" of reality is a dependence on the foundational myths of the Enlightenment — rationalism, scientism, universalism — as the bedrock of cultural judgment, producing a tyranny of fact over value, logic over rhetoric. "It is the search for a way in which one can avoid the need for conversation and deliberation and simply tick off the way things are. The idea is to acquire beliefs about interesting and important matters in a way as much like visual perception as possible — by confronting an object and responding to it as programmed."[3]

To move toward the act of conversation is to move away from this notion that reality and value lie in a "confrontation" with a given object or reality that contains, within itself, a privileged "truth" about its nature and being. Conversation moves away from the temptations of transcendence and teleology toward a notion that cultural value, or the "truth" of art, lies in the contingent relations that come to be constructed through the working out of a particular practice, or in the performative act by which the work at once encounters its audience and constructs its community of interpretation. In the conversationalist view, then, contingency — metaphor and figurative language — must play the part that is attributed, in the confrontational epistemological model, to consequentiality — "realism" and reportage. Where once the metaphors of cultural and social value were derived from the certainty of "causes," Rorty suggests that for our times we should build a cultural imaginary from the experience of art : "A poeticized culture would be one which would not insist we find the real wall behind the painted ones, the real touchstones of truth as opposed to touchstones which are merely cultural artifacts. It would be a culture which, precisely by appreciating that all touchstones are such artifacts, would take as its goal the creation of ever more various and multicolored artifacts."[4] If this sounds like a proposal that merely suggests that "surfaces" are as real as "depths," or proposes an unregulated relativism, then it is important to point out that Rorty is not merely philosophically redescribing the "object" of art, culture, or truth. His contention is that the value we ascribe to objects or practices is no less consequential or effective because their "reality" corresponds less to some immanent "truth" than

2
Richard Rorty, *Philosophy and the Mirror of Nature* (Princeton,. N.J.: Princeton University Press, 1979), 162-63.

3
Rorty, *Consequences of Pragmatism* (Minneapolis: University of Minnesota Press, 1982), 164.

4
Rorty, *Consequences of Pragmatism*, 54.

to the vocabularies through which we describe them and the discourses with which we locate them on the social horizon. "Conversational realities" are not immaculate conceptions or "real" correspondences that satisfy the "eye" of the mind; they are dependent for their authority on the messy, contingent communicability that meshes together a community: "Our identification with our community," Rorty writes, "our society, our political tradition, our intellectual heritage ... is heightened when we see this community as ours rather than nature's, shaped rather than found, one among many which men have made.... [W]hat matters is our loyalty to other human beings clinging together against the dark, not our hope of getting things right."[5]

5
Rorty, *Consequences of Pragmatism*, 166.

This somber image of "conversation" as the community of human survival is not devoid of sustained hope. It is, in fact, the great gift of conversational art to actively engage in the ambivalences and ambiguities that emerge as contextual contingencies from the ironic and contradictory forces that constitute social reality. Taking an antiepistemological stance, the conversationalist develops a discourse that, in attacking "the notion of truth as accuracy of representation [also attacks] the traditional distinctions between reason and desire, reason and appetite, reason and will. For none of these distinctions make sense unless reason is thought of on the model of vision."[6] Contextual contingency, which I see as central to the structure and idea of conversational art, is not opposed to reason. It unsettles the foundational role of reason as the primary source of social and cultural value, while unseating the sovereignty of visuality — reason's mimetic measure — and its advocacy of "accurate" representation as the reproduction, or reflection, of reality. It is by contesting the primacy of reason and its visual analogue that conversation shrinks the distance between subject and object and shatters the cultural silence around the art object. This results in an aesthetic strategy that articulates hitherto unconnected moments between memory and history, revises the traditional divisions between private and public, rearticulates the past and the present, and, through the performance of the artwork, fosters unexplored relationships between historical or biographical events, artistic innovations, and an enlarged sense of cultural community. If, as Rorty says, the confrontational, epistemological approach treats reality as already programmed, then the conversational perspective is at once more provisional, and for that very reason more deeply committed to, the ethical and political "choice" that contingency forces us to be responsible for.

6
Rorty, *Consequences of Pragmatism*, 164.

42

Regina Frank's project, *The Glass Bead Game*, turns my theoretical reflections on conversational art into the experience of live art. If, as I've argued, contextual contingency liberates us from a binary and polarized view that opposes reason to passion, the present to the past, it also commits us to living our lives and making our art from experiences that are ambivalent, contradictory, and unresolved. Such a disturbing, even dark, thought is to be found in the very depths of Frank's project, in the deepest folds of time and memory from which her bead game emerges:

I connected [beads] with certain important events in my life and understood them in a Janus-headed way: connected with luxury and with sorrow, as if these little beads could unify poles of my being. One such personal story, my most important memory of beads, happened two months before my father died. He gave my mother a long string of pearls for her birthday. As she put it around her neck, she said: "Oh, there are so many pearls. I hope this does not mean I will have so many tears." Only later did I realize the connection between this memory and my art, and I started to explore my relationship to beads and pearls as a reflection of my own past.

The Glass Bead Game emerges from a "Janus-headed" experience where beads are at once signs of the presence of love and luxury — pearls — and symbolic of the absence of life — sorrow, tears, death. The pearl necklace is the token of a memory that suddenly, contingently, reveals to Frank the overarching intentionality of her work — without her realizing it: "Only later did I realize...." It is in this initiatory gesture, belatedly recognized, where her own past is revealed through the creative artifice and which she translates into the conversational structure of her installation. She is the subject and object of her own artwork — "both present and absent at the same time" — and it is this game of shifting identifications between art and audience, between history and memory, that becomes the dialectical strategy of her game. Through the intercession of the Internet, the audience "converses" with Frank through virtual beads that transmit messages reflecting on various aspects of the "event": on the work itself, Atlanta and the Olympics, personal experiences, and meditative reflections. Just as Frank was assailed by her deepest memories and experiences through the performance of the artwork, so too is the audience, whose identities are being remade in the very process by which they compose their "moves" in the ongoing play of the bead game:

> Friday July 12, 1996 19:17:35
>
> The secret, hidden text exists
> like a lover, whose trace must be erased,
> like history,
> whose erasures cannot be traced.

> Tuesday, July 30, 1996 19:00:59
>
> I'm a South African art student from Johannesburg....The marks in the sand are important for me because they speak of opposites and the communication or "gap" between these opposites. Namely the process of the trace, the act of healing.

As conversations develop through the fabrication of beads and their encrypted narratives, the gesture of aesthetic communication that I have called contextual contingency emerges to thread together the diversity of bead messages. The messages, as evidenced above, weave the artwork into a digital tapestry of local and global contexts, each time healing the breach of confrontational, binary thinking. At the same time, the bead game demonstrates the transformed environment of cultural representation within which the contemporary artist works — from the craftsmanship of rare Japanese paper cloth and Venetian glass beads, to the computer-generated bead, to the narrative tissue of personal and collective memory. Understanding the value of culture as a texture of experience that will not abide polarities in its attempt to work with the ambivalent and contradictory forces of contemporary culture — the hallmark of a conversational art practice — is precisely what the bead game is about. And in Regina Frank's work we have a distillation of the creative possibilities of contexts — social and aesthetic — that do not necessarily "belong" to each other but have come to coexist contingently, in a way that is strongly suggestive of styles of life and art at the end of our century. "If we concentrate on the essence of the game, it could evoke special powers," writes Frank, "as it is, [quoting Schiller] 'the ingenious unification of reason and lust, intellect and emotions.'"

SHRINKING THE DISTANCE: THE ARTIST AND THE COMMUNITY

Contextual contingency, the defining gesture of conversational art, has particular significance for the place of the artist in the community and the status of the artwork in its address to an audience. The "ingenious unification" of artist and community in the "Conversations" program is, as with the general theory of conversational art, a question of articulating and negotiating cultural and social differences without the promise of some privileged and accurate representation of "totality" or a teleological resolution. The spirit of conversational art lies in initiating "unplanned directions" and provoking "multilayered interpretations," in Jacob's words; this is apparent in the audience's response to, and collaboration with, Regina Frank. They produce bead chains that follow traces that lead from personal testimony to political witnessing, each time acknowledging the pleasure of participating in the making and remaking of the artwork itself. What kind of communal relationship is possible when the artist desires to become, however imperfectly, a member of the community she or he represents? Or when the artwork refuses to respect the "distance" between "subject and object" and the connoisseurial silence that accompanies it?

We have returned to the questions posed at the very beginning of my essay, to move beyond the philosophical implications of a conversational practice and confront its implications for the politics of art and representation. Both approaches share the belief that cultural judgment cannot be founded on a disembodied reading of an image or a sculptural form whose evaluation is based on what Rorty calls "the model of vision," where truth is signified as the accuracy of representation or mimetic "authenticity." The artists in "Conversations" seek an identification with their "subjects" that is profoundly ambitious and ambiguous. Although they are, as a group, as "international" as the cadre of Olympic athletes, "Conversations" skillfully subverts the "nationalist" criteria of cultural representation that informs the international spirit of the Games. The artists who participate in "Conversations" come from a range of countries — Germany, Italy, Ireland, Slovenia, Switzerland, Senegal — but it is neither their national origins nor their pure professional identities that they bring to Atlanta. They do not come in order to make large, nation-based comparisons between Europe and America or East and West. The originality of

44

Bhabha

their projects lies in the common cause sought between the location of the artist as a naturally "displaced" person, often standing on the critical "edge" of society, and those peoples — poor, minoritized, discriminated against — who are consigned to the margins of strongly centralized, powerful metropolitan cultures. In the rage for "global" representation, which increasingly holds the art world in its circular grip as it spins from one international show to another, it is salutary, for instance, to note that Ery Camara chose to identify with Reynoldstown, an African-American area of cultural and community revitalization, and that Dias and Riedweg initiated a dialogue between the inmates of the Fulton County Child Treatment Center and the Atlanta U.S. Federal Penitentiary, because as these artists said, by "exposing fragility or even ignorance we have a possibility of establishing contact with groups of people to which we ourselves do not belong."

One of our most common contemporary self-descriptions is to say that we belong to the "global" village. Advances in digital technologies, the creation of cyberspace, and the international division of labor go some way toward suggesting that we are all members of a brave new global world. But from the local communities we inhabit, the global world still seems full of anxious apprehensions. For as we reach out to touch the new geopolitical surfaces and cultural circumferences that are offered to us through the rhetoric of the "global," we often lose a tangible connection and are thrown back, willy nilly, on cultivating a national perspective in the most effective areas of our lives. This does not mean that we should be Luddites and fail to see what is opening up before us — a world of more complex boundaries, where we are forced to stretch our social and historical imaginations beyond what we can readily visualize or experience. But as we make our global leap — a leap in technology as well as human faith — we must be aware of that early form of globalization, which we have known for the last 250 years as imperialism and neocolonialism. Can the inequalities of power and wealth between the first and third worlds, the north and the south within the West itself, allow us to celebrate the global as if we are all participants in the same local festival? The human family still has its poor relatives, its stepchildren, its orphans. What these ambiguities in the global condition produce are profound anxieties about the way in which we see ourselves as part of a "shared" history of human civilization and barbarism. In a recent essay, the historian of urban experience, Richard Sennett, suggests that we can only properly relate to the global cosmopolitan experience by confronting our deepest anxieties about our own identities and pushing against the ego's narcissistic limits: a real connection to others in the global context "arises from recognizing the insufficiencies of the self … the fractures, self-destructiveness, and irresolvable conflicts of desires within ourselves which … will prompt us to cross boundaries. Openness to the needs of others comes from ceasing to dream of the world made whole."[7]

The art of conversation, as I have suggested, dreams not of the world made whole as much as it emphasizes the need to attend to a world whose making is, at best, a contingent and contradictory enterprise. For this reason "conversation" eschews the vaunting rhetoric of global and local, focusing instead on the problematic of "exclusion" and "inclusion" — that dynamic of

45

7
Richard Sennett, "Christian Cosmopolitanism." *Boston Review* (Oct.–Nov. 1994):13.

Bhabha

marginalization and empowerment that regulates both the global perspective and the local terrain. As the language of globalization threatens to announce a brave new world, it would be well to listen to the community conversations of Camara, for whom, like Sennett, the purpose of conversation is to encounter the lack in ourselves, which then leads to the dialogic desire for the "other" who does not simply fill the gap as much as make possible a process that sloughs off the calloused, dead skin that covers up our vulnerabilities to "difference" — the strange and the unknown — which we parade in a series of stereotypes that circulate, short-sightedly and evasively, as authoritative images. As Camara states:

> One of the rules of conversation is to know how to listen, to receive from someone what is missing in ourselves or to make a link between our sameness and difference. Listening allows a person to better speak or express him- or herself.... It is a constant opposition, and at the same time a transaction, of monologue and conversation, history and memory.

Working within the conversational mode from the perspective of contextual contingency, Camara yokes together oppositional realities and qualities, bringing together various generations of the Reynoldstown community. He constructs his own "bead game" through discussions and art workshops that enable the participants to reflect upon their own "locality" in two important ways: first, to place Reynoldstown in relation to the other cultural communities of Atlanta; and then, to explore and expunge through their own revitalization the dialogue that ensues between groups when the semiotic currency of public discourse is the soiled coin of stereotypy. What emerges in such encounters is the posture of the victim, and Camara's purpose, as I understand it, is to unsettle any such easy identification with the hard lessons of history. For Camara, the aesthetics of "revitalization," whether it applies to a community, a locality, or a tradition of crafts-manship, requires a particular kind of conversational experience that opens itself up to the contingent and paradoxical nature of the dialogic event: "New expressions of relations convert exchanges into living borders. Like seashores renewing the geometry of limits — displacements of time, people, and objects — the whole iconography of paradoxes brings about more perplex-ity." Camara's project enkindles hope in the conversational artifice; Reynoldstown's revitalization is part of a new and emergent identity for the community, one that revises limits and turns dead ends into living borders.

But what of the art of incarceration to which Dias and Riedweg devote their *Question Marks*? I want to conclude my essay with a consideration of Dias and Riedweg's work with people in detention, who are deprived of dialogue and cast out of society because they represent the "limit" case in the aesthetic journey I have undertaken, from the connoisseurial pedagogies of silence to the contingent and contextual practices of conversation. Dias and Riedweg, like Camara, seek to enlarge the possibilities of art's dialogue, its public address, by deploying it to deconstruct stereotypes and displace social territories so that prisoners may, in the public imagi-nation, be drawn out of the prison house of language and prejudice, in which they are incarcer-

46

ated quite beyond their physical detention. Dias and Riedweg enter into this creative undertaking — to represent a social group that has in many ways, renounced its rights of conversation and representation — because of outrage at a quite simple and searing "global" statistic: "Like the United States, about 75 percent of the inmate population in Brazil is black males; in Switzerland, every second inmate is a foreigner. Not only because of our past interests but because of this outrageous reality, we decided to again involve youth in our project in Atlanta."

"[W]hat matters is our loyalty to other human beings clinging together against the dark, not our hope of getting things right."[8] Rorty's words become ever more poignant and urgent when read alongside Dias and Riedweg's description of the "nesting places" the youth inmate-participants imaginatively reconstructed in a series of floorplans. For those who live in the unblinking glare of official surveillance and regulation, the act of drawing a space of their own, marked by the uniqueness and intimacy of a spontaneous everydayness, is a small measure of self-respect regained. Clinging together against the dark develops its own luminous metaphor of communal living. I will let the artists' record take on the story from here:

8
Rorty, *Consequences of Pragmatism*, 166.

> [T]his aspect led to the next idea: the making of a nest, a home, a nurturing and secure place. The youth chose to model their nest on those of the African weaver birds, who share one nest that has many entrances allowing a multitude of birds to occupy individual "cells," as they are referred to. The nest the youth created was made by sewing their memories (about a hundred acetate strips upon which were written questions from their lives) into a huge amorphous structure of coconut fibers. This sculpture eventually found its habitat at The Castle.

47

CODA

Let the nest of African weaver birds, built by the inmates, stand as a monument to the paradoxes of conversational art. It can be read as a double motif, turning the sculpture into a deeply ironic icon for the human need for intimacy and independence, fealty and freedom. From the liberatory perspective, the nest may be the inmates' imagined vision of a community whose diverse points of entry can generously accommodate individuals and groups who represent different interests, even conflicting social passions. Norms would be negotiated, and ethics would be situational and contextual. But the nest is open to another darker reading: that the imagination of the inmates is shaped by the notion of "individual cells"; and there is a sense of conformity and the carceral that clings to the sculpted structure, as if the intimacy of association was based on a fear of the outside world.

The freedom of the conversational critic lies not in choosing the more hopeful, progressive reading while obscuring the obduracy of the negative impulse. For conversation, as I've suggested, depends for its ethical and aesthetic inquiry on living through contradiction and articulating ambivalent interests and identities. Maintaining a belief in a world of bead games and floor plans, which does not accommodate all of humanity, proud and whole, is no less significant for the spirit of survival it embodies and the narrative of endurance it envisages.

Bhabha

ARTISTS' PROJECTS

The Glass Bead Game

REGINA FRANK

den Spieler
Mittelpunkt
eine restlos sy
zufälligen und
haben.»
Jenes Spiel n
bewerb beteilig
logisch aufgebau
auch sich sel
Gespiel it
on als Glas

1996, working on *The Glass Bead Game*, **was a year spent rediscovering long-digested knowledge. This work, created out of conversations for a project in Atlanta and subsequently Tokyo, was an interactive installation in which visitors related stories, poems, quotes, letters, and thoughts to me via the Internet. With a click, they transformed these texts into "virtual beads." Over the course of the installation, I occupied the space and received these beads, created from personal reflections and insights. Some inspired me to choose an actual glass bead from among those I had collected in Venice and ritually affix it into a so-called "magic mantle," connecting thoughts together by fine silk threads. A network of different "thought-beads" now dwells in this multidimensional cloth of communication.**

The transitions from text to texture and poetry to pearls were the main strings tying this piece together. It also resulted in an edition of prints, drawings, a forty-six-minute video, and a web site detailing the process of bead collecting, mantle making, and the game itself. Additionally, a brief video was produced that documented portions of the ritual.

My insights about *The Glass Bead Game* have developed in cycles, since I spent two years researching and creating this piece and was physically present in the installation for more than three months. The beauty of making art for me is the process of seeing, recognizing, and discovering. The dialogue with the audience and critical viewers, as well as friends, and especially with my collaborator Edward Stein and the curator Mary Jane Jacob, influenced its development and my own perception of it. Nearly forty persons collaborated with me and over two thousand contributed with their texts, poems, quotes, letters, and beads. More than any of my past work, *The Glass Bead Game* was the result of many conversations.

52

REGINA FRANK (see pp. 50–51) was born in 1965 and is based in Berlin. Following an apprenticeship in 1986, which culminated in a professional tailor degree, she continued her studies in Berlin, first entering the Department of Asian and Ancient Oriental Studies at the Freie Universät and then the department of visual arts at the Hochschule der Künste, earning an MA in 1993.

Many of her works involve computer technology, often linking the dress as a tactile, female symbol to the virtual world. She made her American debut with *L'Adieu - Pearls Before Gods* (1993) staged in the Broadway window of the New Museum of Contemporary Art, New York. As she worked daily sewing pearls onto a white silk gown, she revealed the relationship of women's labor to the global pay scale. She translated her salary, calculated each day at the rate of a different country, into purchases of bread and flowers — food for the body and soul.

In *Hermes' Mistress*, an ongoing performance project, Frank sits in the middle of a huge, expansive red skirt, working at her portable computer and sewing a spiraling path of letter beads that details information collected from the Internet daily; the artist will continue to fill the skirt with text as she works toward the center of her body. In the beginning she slept underneath it at night like a tent; this aspect led her to rethink the concept of home: home base as home page and dress as address. Begun in 1994, *Hermes' Mistress* has already been performed in Berlin, Bonn, London, Los Angeles, New York, Madrid, and Tokyo.

Other major projects include "Natura Viva" (1995-96), a series of works in which she transmitted thoughts about still life and the transitoriness of information, beauty, blooming, and aging; and *Searching for Babata* (1995-96) in which Frank, under a golden dress, fed her stream of consciousness into the Internet. In addition, Frank has created videos and sites for the World Wide Web and worked as dance performer, clothing designer, and costume and set designer.

Frank is currently working at the shore of the Atlantic Ocean, constructing her own Internet domain and preparing a video-conferencing project that will draw parallels of mental homelessness between the romantic period and today. This project will be accompanied by a series of paintings, drawings, and computer animations inspired by Caspar David Friedrich's painting *The Monk at the Sea* (1810) to be inaugurated in the projects room at "Arco" in Madrid in 1998.

When I search on my computer, I find 35 entries under Mary Jane, 51 under Atlanta, 102 under GBG (for *The Glass Bead Game*), 1,782 related images, 107 Atlanta proposal text notes, 37 budget versions, and more than 2,000 "beads" made from text while *The Glass Bead Game* was on-line and on site. A collection of 828 slides and 252 prints document the process; 28 hours of digital video material and 3.4 gigabytes of digital images were reviewed and edited; 16 hours of taped phone conversations between myself and the curator were recorded between June 18, 1995, and May 30, 1997. Three of these conversations were made from a phone booth in Tokyo because my hotel room didn't provide calling card telephone service. I laugh when I picture myself using the Japanese public phone service, a big file and my computer in front of me, explaining to Mary Jane the changes that *The Glass Bead Game* could take.

In Atlanta, visitors were able to pass their thoughts through a glass window, over broken glass and sand, and enter the game. In the space between myself and the visitors, a video projected on sand showed me collecting favorite lines from books, cutting, twisting, and turning them into threads. These thread-sentences transformed philosophy, literature, and poetry into a cross-cultural weaving, and eventually into the "magic mantle." I did not inhabit this piece of clothing as I had earlier works: dresses as "ad-dresses," as garment and home, as private space and public installation. Instead, it was my goal to fill it with the thoughts of others and create a place for a mental gathering.

The original plan was to collect stories and beads by going around the world. I saw a close relationship between, in my one hand the computer as a carrier of data, a constant component in my life; and in my other hand a custom-made suitcase that also would develop into a carrier of information as it slowly filled with stories or "beads" from different people from different parts of the globe.

Others could have followed the journey beginning and ending in Atlanta, on the World Wide Web, as we traveled to fourteen stations related to historical centers of bead production: Bogota (Columbia), San Salvador (El Salvador), Vancouver (Canada), Seoul (Korea), Manila (Philippines), Denpasar (Bali, Indonesia), Jakarta (Java, Indonesia), Lhasa (Tibet), Abu Dhabi (United Arab Emirates), Addis Ababa (Ethiopia), Lagos (Nigeria), Khania (Crete, Greece), Venice (Italy), and Prague (Czech Republic).

The unexpectedly positive change of plan that followed was influenced by three important factors. First, a travel grant did not come through and cost-saving measures were nearly impossible because prices were inflated by the "Olympic Spirit"; we could not justify conceptually or personally the explosion of production costs that would have been required. Meanwhile, an invitation to be an artist-in-residence at Spiral/Wacoal Art Center, Tokyo, arrived — an opportunity that became interwoven. Finally, the third and most important point was a change of mind.

At that time I was very much thinking and often lecturing about "mental homelessness" caused by the concept of a "global village." From this I developed a form of dress that I used as a shelter and home, literally as "ad-dress." Recentering on the spiritual direction of the Atlanta project made me realize that my traveling around the world was not essential. In fact, its aims might be better met by traveling mentally. I would like to cite the essence from different notes in order to sketch my reflections, an internal conversation that led to this conversion.

Frank

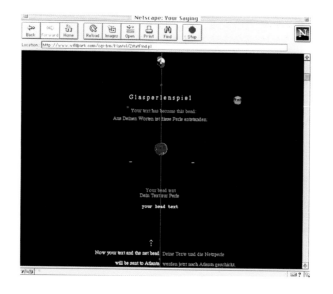

THE JOURNEY

The first step is to think about the different meanings and ways of making a journey. What would happen if the journey around the world happened just in my head? Our most important journeys always take place in our heads.

Travel is to have a conversation with others, to learn from each other, to understand each other's ideas. This links to the original idea of the Olympics as a festival of peace. Peace begins for me with the individual/human concept of community in which an important element is the telling of stories as a global exchange.

If we want to collect beads and their related stories, then why couldn't the story be converted into a bead that exists virtually? If we can travel mentally while we travel in reality, then are we also able to travel mentally in virtual reality?

The speed that we move in an airplane does not correspond to our capability to travel in our minds. We might be present physically in one place, but mentally be in another. My question now is whether we can mentally develop while we physically travel, or will the logistics of the trip, the chasing from one place to the next, not be so consuming that we become physically mobile but mentally stuck?

After picking up my ticket to Tokyo, I dropped off my shoes and had a funny conversation with the Turkish shoemaker. When I asked him to put good soles on my shoes because I had to go around the world to collect beads, his answer was surprisingly straightforward: "Why do you have to go around the world to

Frank

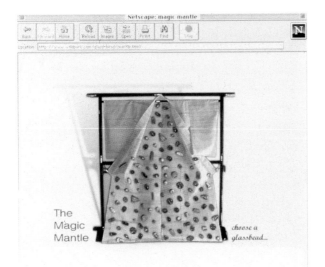

The
Magic
Mantle
                                                        choose a
                                                        glassbead...

find beads when you can buy them around the corner?" At first I laughed and said: "Because the world is not around the corner," but then, I took his advice, went down Kottbusser Tor, and spent an hour in the bead store. Then I went home and browsed through my own cultural background, looking at the books that have been my spiritual companions and with which I have traveled through my life: Greek mythology, fairy tales, Goethe, Faust, Heidegger, Hesse, Wittgenstein, Kant, Musil ... all those German-speaking fellows that hide behind us like a shadow when we start to think in a different language.

I realized that maybe the "dia-logical" step was to bring about a conversion of text, thoughts, stories, conversations. And so, with the development of the concept from travel-in-the-world to travel-in-the-mind, we made a corresponding move away from collecting stories associated with the acquisition of real beads, to the interweaving of stories from my past and the incorporation of the stories of others.

THE MAGIC MANTLE

The man I work with in Berlin to make flowers, lint, and fabric into special paper told me of a Japanese technique to fabricate textiles from paper. This fabric, called *shifu*, was most likely invented in the Tohoku district of Japan where people, unable to afford warm clothing, started to pin paper inside their coats for insulation. Eventually they made it softer by cutting the papers, twisting them into thread and spinning cloth. What originally started as clothing for the poorest has now become something valued more highly than silk. The raw material is cheap, but because the process is so labor intensive the end result is rare and expensive. I e-mailed Spiral Gallery to investigate this in preparation for my first trip to Tokyo.

Frank

The idea was to make a mantle from *shifu* containing my mental journeys. One of these texts, which expresses the desire for a magic mantle, is taken from a conversation between Wagner and Faust; it has impressed me ever since I was a little girl:

> Wagner:
> I'll never envy any bird his wing.
> How differently the joys of spirit bring
> Us on from page to page, from book to book!...
>
> Faust:
> By one impulse alone are you impressed.
> Oh, never learn to know the other!
> Two souls alas! are dwelling in my breast;
> And each is fain to leave its brother....
> Oh, are there spirits hovering near,
> That ruling weave, twixt earth and heaven are rife,
> Descend! come from the golden atmosphere
> And lead me hence to new and varied life!
> Yea! were a magic mantle only mine,
> To bear me to strange lands at pleasure,
> I would not barter it for costliest treasure,
> Not for the mantle of a king resign.

—Johann Wolfgang von Goethe, *Faust*: Part I

The next question was whether I should wear the magic mantle in the performance or whether it would be used as a vessel. This relates essentially to my questions about dwelling and homelessness (better in German, *Unbehaustsein*; or in Ge-nglish, *unhomebeing*). It seemed more dia-logical to inhabit this mantle with the "words" of others and link each thought converted into a bead to another, since my own presence was already in the texture of the fabric (p. 57).

BEADS AND THEIR LINKS

Beads are probably the oldest objects of beauty in cultural history. As beads generally had an intimate relationship with their owners, they are often found as grave goods in the earliest burials. Old beads are little carriers of secrets containing more information than just age, material, and place of origin. We could call beads the "change of civilization" as they are indicative of exchange — giving information about trading relationships, technological standards, and the culture of communities.

The bead, as a mirror of culture that reflects social, political, economic, and religious life, is at the center of this project. In its kaleidoscopic variability the bead creates a perfect unit.

During my childhood I was fascinated by the stories I linked to beads. I connected them with certain important events in my life and understood them in a Janus-headed way: connected with luxury and with sorrow,

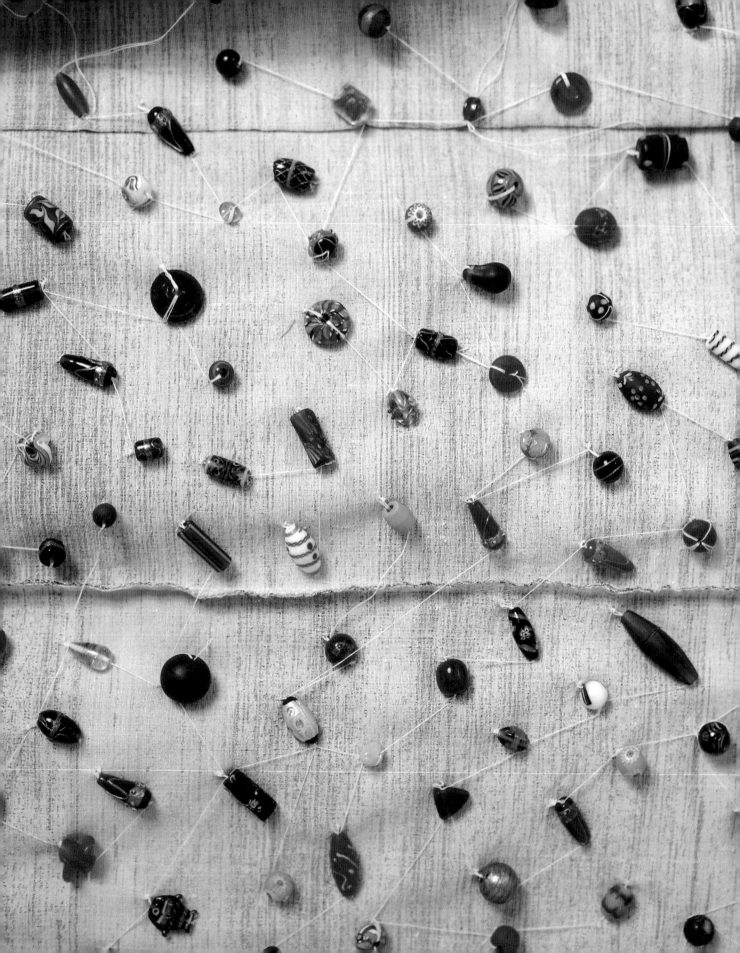

as if these little beads could unify poles of being. One such personal story, my most important memory of beads, happened two months before my father died. He gave my mother a long string of pearls for her birthday. As she put it around her neck, she said: "Oh, there are so many pearls. I hope this does not mean that I will have so many tears." Only later did I realize the connection between this memory and my art, and I started to explore my relationship to beads and pearls as a reflection of my own past.

BEADS, GLASS, AND SAND

As I see beads as carriers of information, I see glass as their material, sand as their substance. Thus, sand as a carrier of information symbolizes the transitory nature of information and the impossibility to grasp it as a phenomenon.

Interestingly, silicon chips are made from refined sand, and, though a natural material, they can be viewed as an integral part of a complex information system, paralleling the binary structure of digitally coded information. Writing in sand corresponds to writing at the computer screen; letters dissolve with the next wave of thought, just as waves convert millions of shells back into tiny particles.

I see the glass window as a parallel to the computer window: both protect, leading into the installation and providing in-sight; and reflect outward, creating a distance in which viewers are forced to discover their own insights and stories, intellectually and/or emotionally. Confronted with one's own reflection, these windows become a second layer within the installation tableau.

Broken glass with sand covers the main floor of the installation. It reminds me of broken windows, a broken inside, a broken insight, broken ice, or, conversely, the expression "the ice is broken," when conversation melts away the divisions of communication. This reminds me, too, of the fairy tale "The Snow Queen" in which Kai sits in the queen's castle playing the "game of wisdom." There, completely remote from the rest of the world, he creates words from pieces of ice, trying to find "eternity." "Blinded" by a splinter from a mirror, he saw little imperfections as big problems; his focus on details made him lose sight of the value of the whole. Likewise, obsessed by one's field, one can dwell on tiny matters that are unimportant to others or may be insignificant in the larger realm of life. Getting lost in details, we often forget where we are in our world — our position as a bead in the chain of life.

THE GLASS BEAD GAME AND ITS LINKS

The title of the project is taken from Hermann Hesse's 1943 novel, which attempts to describe the life of Magister Ludi (the glass bead game master) Josef Knecht and his growing success as a master of intellectual connections among a spiritual elite, the non-confessional community called Castalia. Knecht embodies the highly intellectual human being who, in seeking the Whole, finally drowns in the conflict between his worldly and spiritual life. The *Ludus Sollemnis*, the glass bead game, which takes place once a year, represents the peace between the different disciplines and evokes the memory of the Whole that rules the units. For its players it is almost religion, meditation, the celebration and manifestation of art, and the *creator spiritus*.

In this context, to me, Hesse's glass bead game is like a spiritual Olympic game: it creates a peace through which there can be an exchange among different peoples; it is a convening of different faculties in an

58

atmosphere of playfulness and joy. For the global exchange of many different interests with relative ease, the Internet seemed a perfect playground for a glass bead game. If we concentrate on the essence of the game, it could evoke special powers, as it is "the ingenious unification of reason and lust, intellect and emotions" (Friedrich Schiller).

It was originally forbidden for professionals to participate in the Olympic Games, because the Olympic committee thought that earning money would interfere with the Olympic spirit of play. The true player doesn't play for victory. In Hesse's glass bead game there is no winner but rather a master of the game, who finally loses interest in the game because it is too remote from the world.

THE GLASS BEAD GAME, GERMAN LANGUAGE, AND HISTORY[1]

Hesse completed *The Glass Bead Game* in increasing political frustration. The reality of contemporary events, the rise of Hitler, and the horrors of Nazism opened Hesse's eyes to the failure of the intellectuals and convinced him of the futility of a spiritual realm divorced from contemporary social reality. In the chapter "A Conversation," Hesse's protagonist (Knecht) realizes while debating with a representative of the outside world (Plinio Designori) that a life devoted exclusively to the mind is not only not fruitful but also dangerous. His conclusion was to give up his position in Castalia, which he justified as follows: "Here I am sitting in the top story of our Castalian edifice, occupied with the glass bead game, working with delicate, sensitive instruments, and instinct tells me, my nose tells me, that down below something is burning and that my business is not to analyze music or define rules of the Game, but to rush to where the smoke is."

Basing an artwork on a piece of German literature was accompanied by a personal discomfort, since my relationship to my mother language has always been shadowed by Germany's — our — history. The reading of my favorite books in English translation was a very important part of the process. Converting those quotes into texture, tediously turning the German words and digesting them into a piece of history that one can wear, felt like a release and liberation.

RE- AND INTER-ACTIONS

I stayed in my tableau during the course of the exhibition, hoping to evoke different thoughts about games as part of our social life. I played with the visitors, was part of the image, was a medium, a recipient for the audience. I was surrounded by sand, glass, beads, the mantle, quotes, and technology. My technological clones (me in the video producing the magic mantle and me as part of the computer poetry-bead-making program) competed with me for attention; I was both present and absent at the same time. Ironically, while people were writing to me, they were so completely absorbed by the screen and the keyboard that my movements went unnoticed. My cage-like enclosure made me feel at times like an animal in a natural history museum; or was I watching the audience without them realizing that they were the ones being watched?

Once a message was sent and the text transformed into a bead, it was up to me to pull the thread and react to the message. I had the option to drop the bead and ignore it or to play a dialogical game. I was conscious of those beads as carriers of information, as thoughts that had been going through many different people's

1
The German word for glass bead game, Glasperlenspiel, is for me a metaphor for the glory and tragedy of culture in our time. German offers the possibility of "building" words by simply pasting them together. In the past the totalitarian system of Nazism used this to invent a whole new language to cover over its most horrifying intentions. If we think separately of Reich (kingdom, country, but also rich), Kristall (crystal, glass), and Nacht (night), one would have difficulty imagining that the "richcrystalnight" (Reichskristallnacht) could be a word to describe the beginning of one of the cruelest, most incomprehensible periods of hatred and cultural intolerance. I doubt that it is merely coincidental that more than half a century later, in 1989 on the same date — the 9th of November — a second layer of history was used to melt away this memory, shattering two very different political moments into one: the dismantling of the Mauer (the Berlin Wall, as it was called on the west side) or the antifaschistischer Schutzwall (the antifascist protection wall, as it was called on the east). Linking words creates and changes meaning. Language has influenced the development of culture. Maybe by understanding different meanings and the overlaying of meanings through history, we can gain an understanding and tolerance of cultural differences.

Saturday, June 29, 1996 15:48:38
In 1980 the U.S. boycotted the Olympics in the
Soviet Union because the Soviets invaded Afghanistan.
In 1996 the Olympics are in my front yard but
Afghanistan is still in my heart — broken and bleeding.
Author: Shifalo

Sunday, June 30, 1996 18:32:20
The terror and delight of the universe needs an
unpiercable cloak. Woven of nettles and reeds from
the banks of the Tigris. She immerses herself in a
bath of beads every night, it is conducive to
meditation. Only in this way can she achieve the
serenity to deal with her mother who thinks she knows everything.
Author: Lily Yancey

Sunday, June 30, 1996 23:14:35
SWEATING ENTOMBED AND ENSHRINED WITHIN ONE EYE
SPY MORE ON SHADOWED SHORES OUT OF THIS WORLD
WITHIN ONE BEAD
ITS PUPIL=3D ITS BRAIN+
ITS GLASS COCOON TRANSLUCENT MOON
IF ONLY TO MOVE TO EXPLORE TO BREATH AND TO
SLOBBER — THIS COULD BE WATER A DROP FROM THE SKY
AND WITHIN IT I AM AS WEAK AS IT IS SOLID KNOWING
ALAS IT IS GLASS NOW
SHATTERED
WHOLE AND FREE
I SEE SHARDS IN MY SKIN
RELEASED I FIND MY KIN
Author: BONECOIL

Thursday, July 4, 1996 20:13:42
As frustrating as weaving sometimes is for me,
it is as close to a meditation as I have ever gotten.
Once I start to weave, all the problems
I may have had with the warp seem to disappear
and, temporarily, my own problems as well.
Author: Bonnie Kelemen

Wednesday, July 10, 1996 18:43:44
The Hesse quote had good linkage with me. My
work is understanding consumer behavior and
attitudes and transforming those intangibles into
more tangible things that can be acted
upon ... like improving products and creating new
things that people say they want. The
juxtaposition of the intangible thought and the
tangible product of thought is special. I hope to come back
to your work to see it again, Danke.
Author: JT

Wednesday, July 10, 1996 23:24:05
Hi I am one of your regulars, until now
I see you every day —
the first time I was caught on the street
by my own reflection, the next thing I know
is I stumble into this magic installation,
lose orientation
projections, Japanese letters
she is cutting her books, spinning, weaving
then I discover you
in the background
so strange — sitting in your black dress
typing, fast — black magic woman,
through the binoculars I see your pupils
wandering over the computer screen
your eyes like your magic beads — rolling
your appearance
like a summer snow queen and pitch marie
Is the broken glass a broken illusion
suddenly you get up, it's like a dance
you're deleting some writings in the sand
playing a game with magic
brushes sticks beads mantles
what are you dreaming about
that it feels so secret and far away from today
unreachable you behind the glass
you start to be in my dreams
this morning I sit at my computer, feel I should write you
I try to come by this afternoon again
I am scared to come back, on Sunday you gave me
a smile from far away, behind the glass,
I wonder how your voice sounds
I wish you'd always stay
Author: Andrew

Saturday, July 13, 1996 19:31:14
Here I live, jostling & tricky
in the blue descriptive city
I have been here too, many times before you
and now it's time to go
crazy again. Will that make you like me?
I think so
often about you, all the bon beads we had
wanted to have, but didn't?
I didn't ask for this
I asked for you but saw myself
Reflected in the glass, broken
and whole and clear. Through all this distance
I wish you were near.
Author: Parker Wheatly

Saturday, July 13, 1996 20:34:28
Life should be as calm and quiet as you seem to
be writing in the sand
Author: Anita

Friday, July 12, 1996 19:17:35
The secret, hidden text exists
like a lover,
whose trace must be erased,
like history,
whose erasures cannot be traced.
Author: Pam Longobardi

Friday, July 12, 1996 21:39:07
Every day I cross the line that separates me from
you. Sometimes the line is a fence, sometimes
the line is fiber optic cable, sometimes it is shattered glass.
I continue to reach across the boundaries —
natural and manmade — to make contact with
someone on the other side.
Author: Abla Hamilton

Sunday, July 28, 1996 00:55:50
The beads symbolize to me the power of diversity,
which is actually a great source of creativity.
This is so important on this day in light of the
bombing in Centennial Park. Diversity and creativity
need to be embraced now more than ever before.
Authors: Todd, Susan, and Scott

Tuesday, September 10, 1996 05:33:54
I brought you today three button-beads from my
favorite piece of clothing. I wore this dress for
ten years after my mother bought it for me. Last
year I decided that the dress looks too shabby,
because there were too many holes, so I started
to wear it as a night gown. This year after
mending the dress several times I cut it apart to
put it together into a patchwork blanket. The
dress had 20 buttons, from which I keep 17,
three are for you as a present for your magic
mantle. The other 17 I will keep together with the
the good spirit of my past ten happy years.
Author: Mayumi Onouchi

Saturday, July 27, 1996 22:07:21
I always thought of glass beads as being thin
spindles of glassine impervious and cold until
warmed by the palm ... and I see erasures upon the
sand, a sweeping clean of time like a cold ocean,
the hand and fingers of God ... and I saw a lovely
woman in a store window in Soho selling time ...
it's selling time like it's something that can be tallied and
bartered away but we all know time is a gift that flies
and flies its engravings left upon our fingers to warm
the hours and drill the unknowing,....
Author: Christopher Kuhl

Saturday, August 3, 1996 00:02:57
Such a magical creation comes more strongly from
the voices of many than of one, the voices of
many nations, many realities, many individuals.
Author: LM Gaudet

Thursday, September 12, 1996, 11:38:19
In Tokyo the airplane landed, I looked into
the daylight and lit a cigarette. How is it that I should
look into the future rather than the present?
I continued my journey long in to the darkness
when the cityscape turned blue. The moon
became noon and amongst the shadow of neon lights I
became aware that I was a child. There was
laughter in the distance, I was overcome by a
certain uncontrollable desire to sleep. It then
became noon. As I lick my lips, there is no
place to turn no exit no back no front no sky no earth.
I keep walking but the city became endless.
This story continues at the end.
Author: Rirkrit Tiravanija

Tuesday, July 30, 1996 19:00:59
I'm a South African art student from
Johannesburg. Your work interests me as I find the
notion of trace compelling. The way the needle
penetrates the fabric, not destructively, but with
healing qualities. Processes of weaving seem to be
the "gap" between states of chaos and healing.
The marks in the sand are important for me because
they speak of opposites and the communication
or "gap" between these opposites. Namely the process
of the trace, the act of healing.
Author: Taryn Millar

hands and minds, rolling though different fingers, some worn out and pale, others new and shiny.

Thoughts — beads — if I drop one, it is like a conversation; you only hear what touches you and what you can catch from the other. Some time later, one of these disregarded pearls rolls in front of you, then you remember and suddenly discover its beauty.

Often people made reference to the Olympic Games, to the poetry of the piece, daily political developments, or to their own experience in exploring the installation. Most of the viewers observed the piece as an environment, which they explored calmly, often in more than one visit and making more than one bead. Employees from the adjacent AT&T building, who came over during their lunch breaks, sent me beads from their computers or from "out of town." They could find out whether their bead had been published on the web site, see how many other people had made beads since they had, search for authors they knew, and even react to other beads. Perhaps it was the participatory aspect that encouraged them to stay longer and come more often. This was the kind of engagement only experienced when you allow a certain conversational interaction to occur, so that the visitor is not just a consumer but becomes present in the environment.

People began to care about me, imported me into their private lives, and established personal relationships. Some used me as a confession machine or as a "garbage can" for their souls; others reminded me of the existence of supernatural powers or wanted to convert me to believe in Jesus. Most people were proud to contribute to the mantle, to be part of the environment, and to have their thoughts represented by a bead. Often there was enough curiosity to involve the house manager Becky Reynolds or my collaborator

Frank

Edward Stein in long chats. Some men developed an almost flirtatious relationship with me but were strangely uncomfortable when we met accidentally outside the installation. A woman who had been there with her husband came back alone and made a very powerful bead; she stayed for about three hours. Several days later I saw her again with her husband, this time leading a group of people through the installation. She still writes me sometimes, although we have never actually spoken.

For many people the dialogue was quiet. Receiving their intimate lines, I most often communicated with my own sign language by drawing in the sand, as most of the beads were touching me close to my skin. Grateful, I would pick up a single bead and place it in a silent dialogue with other beads in the magic mantle.

The Glass Bead Game **made me realize the potential of conversation to initiate conversion, transformation, change of heart, or even metamorphosis.**

My favorite quotes from the past, once communicated, were converted into threads — a textured memory. The quotes of others had to go through a similar transition by being converted into glass beads. Symbolically, they stood for conversation by which thoughts are transformed, transmitted, and converted into something else — transporting something personal from one person to another.

Frank

IRWIN Live and
Transnacionala: A Journey from the East to the West Coast
IRWIN

The two projects we presented in Atlanta were based on the idea of movement and the exploration of time in two different directions. *IRWIN Live* **was a subjective work, oriented inward and into the past.** *Transnacionala* **dealt with the idea of movement through time, oriented outward and into the future.**

The references for *IRWIN Live* were from the history of art and its formal questions. Its framework consisted of: the object (paintings), the body (the five IRWIN members hanging in performance, then replaced by dummies during the exhibition), space (rotated by ninety degrees), and an audience (visitors viewing an exhibition of an exhibition). *IRWIN Live* was a reflection of art as it has been practiced by the IRWIN group, making visible the act of us looking at our first collaborative work, a series of our paintings from 1984, appropriately entitled "Was ist Kunst?" (pp. 64–65). For "Conversations at The Castle," we inverted the conventional parameters of viewing in a gallery by shifting the paintings from wall to ceiling. Thus, the audience watched the viewing of paintings rather than the paintings themselves. The experience we encountered while hanging just about a meter above the heads of the audience was a physical and mental change in the perception of oneself. Because sound moves horizontally, we didn't hear any voices in spite of the viewers' close proximity; neither did we see anyone, as we had our backs turned to the audience. All this created the feeling that we were actually being exhibited. Yet in a certain way we were invisible, too, as though in a different temporal dimension or maybe even occupying our own past.

The aesthetic and ethical point of departure of *Transnacionala* was the very implementation of the project itself, our attempt to establish complex personal and group experiences within a time-space module, and the effort to live within a multitude of linguistically indefinable connections. Our primary motive was to organize an international art project that would take place outside established institutional networks, without intermediaries, curator-formulated concepts, or any direct responsibility to sponsors.

IRWIN, (pp. 64-65) founded in 1983 in Ljubljana, Slovenia, consists of painters Dušan Mandic (born in Ljubljana, 1954), Miran Mohar (born in Novo Mesto, 1958), Andrej Savski (born in Ljubljana, 1961), Roman Uranjek (born in Trbovlje, 1961), and Borut Vogelnik (born in Kranj, 1959). One of the founding member groups of NSK – Neue Slowenische Kunst (New Slovene Art) — an artistic organization established in 1984, IRWIN defines its activities as based on "emphasized eclecticism" and "retro principle." Their first work, "Was ist Kunst?," was a series of paintings conceived as a means of realizing the coexistence of various artistic styles: from the tradition of historical avant gardes through popular imagery to the visual production of the totalitarian regimes. In the 1990s this ongoing project has focused on the question of the status of the art object.

In 1992 IRWIN moved to a more conceptual phase with the formation of the "NSK State in Time" through the *NSK Embassy* and *NSK Consulate* projects, specific social installations that symbolically and artistically transfer the phenomenon of NSK into other cultural, social, and political contexts. The first *NSK Embassy* (1992) was realized in Moscow and documented in the book *NSK Embassy Moscow: How the East Sees the East* (1993). Subsequent *NSK Embassies* were opened in Ghent, Berlin, and Sarajevo at the National Theater; *NSK Consulates* were opened in Florence in the Hotel Ambasciatori and in Umag, Croatia, in the kitchen of the private apartment of gallery owner Marino Cettina. The *NSK Passport Office* project has been presented by IRWIN independently and within the framework of larger projects such as *Transnacionala*. In IRWIN's 1996 exhibition entitled "Interior of the Planet" (Museum Boijmans Van Beuningen, Rotterdam), selected works from "Was ist Kunst?" were shown in two specially designed containers along with an architectural model of the "NSK State in Time" and a film presenting NSK members' ideas about art. The audience was transported through the show by the *NSK Vehicle*, an electric car equipped with a TV monitor on which visitors could watch a curator-guided tour. This exhibition was subsequently shown in the Ludwig Museum, Budapest (1996), and at Tramway, Glasgow (1997). After undertaking *Transnacionala* in the United States, IRWIN prepared an exhibition of the same title in which they presented related works and unedited video material documenting the journey's discussions. This exhibition was also shown at the Kunstverein, Hamburg; La Caixa, Barcelona; Galerija Dante, Umag; and Inge Baecker Gallery, Cologne. A book and a film on *Transnacionala* are currently in preparation.

In short, we wanted to organize a project as a direct network of individuals brought together by a common interest in dealing with aesthetic, ethical, social, and political questions spontaneously and without any predetermined or centralized aesthetic, ideological, or political objective. We would travel together for one month, exchange views, opinions, and impressions, meet new people in their local environments, and try to expand the network of conversation around the topicality of questions posed.

Our second methodological point of departure was to create conditions for a kind of experimental existential situation. Like *NSK Embassy Moscow* (our one-month stay in a Moscow apartment on Leninsky Prospekt 12), the one-month cohabitation of ten individuals in two motor homes barely ten square meters in size (p. 68) was designed to problematize the myth of the public versus the intimate or private aspects of artist and art, a split that forms the basis for the system of representation. The fifteen embassies and consulates of NSK (*Neue Slowenische Kunst*), including *Transnacionala*, emanate from the concept of a "state in time": a "state" of mind whose borders fluctuate according to the movements and changes of its symbolic and physical collective body. Thus, our work is state art in the service of a state without territory.

NSK Embassy Moscow: How the East Sees the East was staged as part of the "Apt-Art" (Apartment Art) project in 1992 and coincided with and marked the moment of transformation in Eastern Europe — a transformation not only of a political nature but one that reached into all segments of existence. This communication project emerged out of the need to face the task of reflecting on our totalitarian past in order to prepare for life in societies-in-transformation. *Transnacionala* grew out of the positive outcome of this project and included three of our Russian artist-friends from that project: Alexander Brener, Vadim Fishkin, and Yuri Leiderman. However, the Atlanta project essentially differed from the Moscow experience in that it represented a confrontation with America, a society quite unlike ours, and yet, through media and global corporations, one that is present in all societies in the world today. Because we were experiencing America as outsiders and because it is a nation formed through constant movement — a country of highways and of migration — we decided not to repeat the previous form (say, setting up an embassy in New York or another big city) but to enter this American experience through the idea of motion.

The form we chose for *Transnacionala* was the journey — a journey from the East to the West Coast. A move, a walk, a journey, all indicate inner — either individual or collective — transformation; these passages presume a substantial change or the need to change from one state of matter to another. Journeys have historic as well as mythological references: Christian pilgrimages, traveling around the world, the Grand Tour, summit ascents of the world's highest mountains, the Olympic marathon of the torch bearer, the migration of nations, the travels of beatniks along Route 66. American culture is constantly on the move, which is not typical of other, older civilizations. This is why American popular myths are often based on the idea of travel, conquest, the thirst for new experience, a "new" world. Through our journey we came to better understand these myths. A journey across America is a kind of a modern archetype. It reaches into the very idea of the discovery and colonization of America. Through *Transnacionala* we established direct contact with the fundamental mechanisms of the myth making that had determined our ideas and dreams of America since childhood, such diverse realms as Westerns, Karl May, American art after World War II, and the events surrounding 1968.

IRWIN

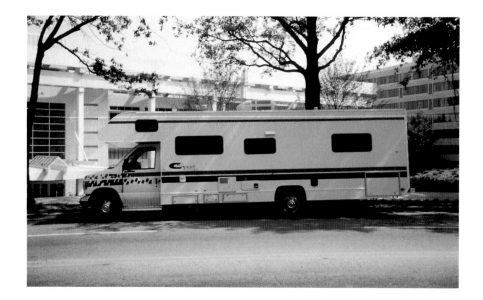

Our journey was comprised of discussions, presentations, and public and private events beginning in Atlanta and staged sequentially in Richmond, Chicago, San Francisco, and Seattle in cooperation with hosts Mary Jane Jacob, Katherine Gates, Randy Alexander, Charles Kraft, Robin Held, and Larry Reed. The project also existed in the wider information network and in symbolic form: via the Internet (pp. 70, 71), reports were made en route and video letters mailed to The Castle and the concurrent "Manifesta" exhibition in Rotterdam, where they were made available to visitors as part of the *NSK Vehicle*. *Transnacionala* will also be interpreted by American documentary filmmaker Michael Benson and in a book by the IRWIN group.

How to conceptualize "post festum" an artistic event that took place in individual and collective consciousness, in a flow of thoughts and emotions largely determined by the very corporality and directness of events, vanishing in time as the journey progressed mile by mile, from city to city, from meeting to meeting?

The nondifferentiated, subjective material of *Transnacionala* that the journey's participants brought back home is a kind of amalgam of images, impressions, memories, and realizations. The banalities of everyday life (which included sleeping, eating, cleaning the crowded living environment and ourselves, psychological tensions, and attempts to relax) all intertwined with the more sublime impressions of unforgettable landscapes, wide expanses, and people; with reflections physically linked to these different normal or exalted states; with memories of conversations, towns, and the atmospheres in which they took place; as well as with tentative syntheses occasioned by thought-shifts between different time, space, and existential zones — between America, Europe, and the world; between memories of local life situations in Ljubljana, Moscow,

New York, and Chicago — all caught up in the dull gaze and the monotonous image that defined for hours and hours, the content and basic situation of the motor homes. Although it is difficult to move beyond this nondifferentiated image, impression, and experience of *Transnacionala*, the months that have elapsed since the project ended in Seattle on July 28, 1996, provide a sufficient "time-distance" to produce at least a rough reckoning of what the direct experience of the project signifies with respect to its initial conceptual points of departure as they were developed out of the strategies of *NSK Embassy Moscow.*

Based on our East European background, the basic question repeatedly posed to the American public present at our events was: What does the American cultural public understand by the notions of the East — of Eastern art, of Eastern societies? (What already exists in the minds of our interlocutors?) On the other hand, we were faced with the question of how to present our real aesthetic, existential, and historical experience in such a way as to transcend the cultural, ideological, and political headlines linked to the collapse of Eastern political systems and the wars in the former Yugoslavia and former Soviet Union. How to define cultural, existential, and historical differences in the context of global, transnational capitalism? And finally, how to transcend sociological discourse and establish conditions for aesthetic discourse?

Communicating with various American art and intellectual communities revealed a certain similarity between the attitudes, even the frustrations, of various American minority groups (based on national, cultural, racial, sexual, religious, or ideological identity) toward the activity of mainstream social institutions and the frustration of East European cultures in relation to their economically stronger West European and North American counterparts (in other words, the relation of the margin to the center). When mentioning this relationship, attitude, or simple frustration toward the prevailing world order as a point of potential identification within the context of difference, we primarily had in mind the semiconscious, ambivalent, and nonstructured nature of the language used to structure public dialogue around the following questions: Who are we? Who and what do we represent? Who am I? Who and what do I represent? These questions gradually gained in importance, giving the project a kind of ontological stamp precisely because of their ambivalence and insolubility.

None of us, as so-called East European artists, identified with the East in the sense of representing its political or even cultural messianic role. Our common attitude to this question could be defined as an attempt to take a different view, to formulate different questions: How does the East see itself from the outside, from the point of view of another continent, and what constitutes its role and place in the structure of the global world order? What remains of ourselves and our conceptual and aesthetic points of departure once we are transposed into a foreign cultural and historical context? Who are we by ourselves? Can art really contextualize and interpret itself through itself? From where do form and content derive? Does autonomy — freedom of art and the individual — exist? If it does, on what values is it based?

These seemingly direct, even worn out and abused, questions brought about numerous conflicts, deadlocked discussions, retreats into silence and reflection, depressions, exalted visions of solutions, utopian impulses, feelings of absurdity, emptiness, and exposure to the mechanisms of life. In the middle of the desert, where all points of the universe seem equally close to and equally distant from man, we were discovering that as East European artists we were not defined so much by the form and content of our mental spaces as by their symbolic exchange value.

IRWIN

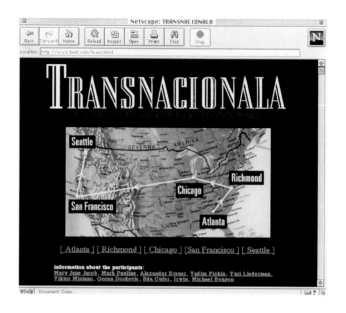

Meeting with American artists, we found their outlook on art tagged by social conditions. Certain formal solutions present in American art are only partially acceptable to those who do not live in the reality that enables these solutions. Due to differing contexts, communication was often chaotic; at other times it reached the highly focused level of reciprocal exchange. Thanks to the uncommon motive and form of this project, authentic forms of communication emerged as we located mutual interests that connected us to their existence as well as to the models in which they live and within which they create. Meeting different individuals and groups during the journey we, by ourselves, constituted a paradigm of the public, functioning like any other marginalized community, galvanized around our identity and shared histories.

Far away from our usual way of living, we understood more than ever before the frustration of Eastern cultures and societies vis-à-vis Western ones, which grew even bigger after the collapse of socialism and are manifest in the field of art primarily as the problem of the nonexistence of a system of contemporary art in the East. We lack a system of symbolic and economic exchange that could pave the way for integration into the global contemporary art system.

But why would we regret the nonexistence of something suppressing the individual and his artistic freedom, at least according to the romantic, utopian definition of art? Even today its demise is still formally advocated by a great number of ideologues and users of the existing West European and U.S. system of contemporary art. Ours is not regret but a realization that without a system of institutions that, by definition, represent the field of contemporary art, there is no broader intellectual and creative production. Without broader intellectual and creative production, there are no differences; without differences, there

IRWIN

is no hierarchy of values; without a hierarchy of values there is no critical reflection; without critical reflection, there is no theory; and without theory, there is no universally understood referential language capable of communicating on an equal footing with other referential languages in other places and times.

The aim of our research, too, was to analyze the values and problems of the global art system, its existential, linguistic, and market models. The problem, as we see it, is specifically the power that decides whether a particular individual or collective art production is a "real" part of the public exchange of values or merely what could be termed the "hyper-production" of an alienated artist, unclaimed in his or her studio, stuck in the cellar or attic of a private house, in the inventory of a bankrupt gallery, in a collection that has lost its value overnight, or in some other of history's many dumping grounds.

The structure of the artist-art-audience triad in today's art world system is primarily conditioned by the strategies of mediators — curators, gallerists, collectors, critical theorists. By willfully avoiding the mediator, *Transnacionala* tried to introduce a change in the understanding of these relationships. The end of the second millennium is at hand and the dynamics of global change are immense; we believe that the relationships among artist, art, audience, the art system, and the categories on which they are based will be redefined.

One type of relationship with the public is letting artworks be looked at, watched, commented upon, interpreted; we as artists participate in this indirectly by objectifying ourselves in our work. A second type of relationship to the public is to search for a direct, corresponding audience. In the case of *Transnacionala*, we had two such audiences: we as participants in the journey observing the artwork as we were forming it;

IRWIN

and those who joined us in the structure set forth in the various cities through which we moved. Thus, there were "private" conversations taking place within the group and "public" conversations with persons encountering a group of artists about whom, for the most part, they had no prior information. Our goal was not merely to introduce our work but rather to frame it within the historical and social context from which we came, and then to compare this context with those typical in the United States.

On the surface, *Transnacionala* may seem yet another attempt to establish or reaffirm the myth of communication. Its mission could be defined as an attempt to bridge personal, cultural, ideological, political, racial, and other differences. It was, in fact, in this positive, optimistic spirit that the first letters to participants and hosts were composed. Frequently such an agitprop discourse was also used in establishing communication with the public in the five American cities visited. It is more difficult, however, to define how and with what complications this communication really took place. The success of communication among individuals from different cultures and with different experiences depends primarily on the skill of the individuals and groups desiring to communicate, skill at playing a role within the structure of a dialogue.

In the context of contemporary art and theory, the role of the engineer of such a communication structure is largely played by international institutions, intermediaries who have maintained the illusion, despite cultural, political, economic, and individual differences, that the contemporary art community speaks the same language. Since the 1970s collapse of the "option of the Left" (which determined the value system and consistency of language on which that illusion was based), this communication framework has been showing its cracks and fissures. It has shown itself inadequate, yet it remains the only model linking disparate individuals and groups, protecting them from sinking back into more or less primitive national and local communities.

By trying to circumvent the institutional framework and ignore the potential of skillful professionals who would inevitably try to place the event within an established context of reception, the *Transnacionala* project deliberately provoked what could be called "communication noise." It placed the event in a certain margin where it became a subject of scrutiny, provoking questions about the point of the participants' own activity, about what made the project different from a tourist trip abusing national and international art funds in the interest of structuring pleasure. At times the participants saw themselves as a bunch of demoralized, neurotic individuals in pursuit of abstract private utopias, nonexistent relations, and deficiencies for which there can be no compensation. These feelings gradually took on the status of a unique experience, of a state we had deliberately provoked. They became the subject and theme of the journey.

Communication took place on various conflicting levels as individuals brought their own subjects and interests into the relationship. Despite bringing up problems that promised no imminent solutions and despite communication that lacked colloquial smoothness (that was, in fact, at times full of clashes and thorns), *Transnacionala* **achieved its conceptual objective precisely by objectifying itself in the sphere of intimacy and closeness, which in the process of the journey took on the form of a microcosm of public space. It also embraced a public space in which views of contemporary art that are still considered taboo in most public contexts could be expressed.**

Among the participants of the journey and other individuals along the way, relationships were established, forming a direct, living network in which a sum of problems and realizations constituting the germ of a new, referential language were caught and articulated in order to be developed further.

IRWIN

73

From Monologue to Conversation
ERY CAMARA

My work developed out of an invitation to critically analyze the relation between audiences and cultural institutions. Institution must be understood here to be a hierarchical structure organized in order to reach objectives, aims, or power, the impact of which can be measured. Research, design, display — all the strategies applied by institutions such as museums and galleries — have to be reconsidered as layers, edges, and nets, that is, as ideological apparatuses. These are used by those in power — the ruling classes — to increase knowledge and affect cultural behavior within communities, reshaping and legitimizing what generations have understood and understand as civilization.

Museum exhibitions are a discourse, a mirror, a reflection that owners, sponsors, staff, and sometimes the state use for their own interests, applying a criteria of power that can include or exclude whoever does not fit in the framework. So, according to our background and references, viewers are able to be located and are allowed either to interact or only to follow the established rules. Let us stress that resistance to these policies is another discourse. People are also institutions, or part of them, according to their disciplines, training, and the organization of interventions that shift boundaries in culture. The approach of the institution and the audience shows us that the means of communication between authorities and the public can provoke active interaction or just audience consumption of what is offered.

The history of African-Americans, as with the history of many minorities, can be illustrated by its interpretation, presence, and manipulation in museums. These distorting mirrors bring back the myth of Narcissus or Snow White's stepmother queen, both representing monologue and self-praise in a naming and categorizing process. Historians have stated that African-Americans have been denied a historic and artistic background, though their collective memory contradicts these statements. Their awareness of a pertinent cultural background allows them to re-create and harmonize their past and present in an original way, a living reality. But it is important to observe that the monologue that excluded them also creates self-exclusion. The power that controls media, material needs, education, and many corporate policies of production and distribution exclude those who cannot afford the amount of knowledge, currency, or class required to become a welcome member. Thus, African-Americans are isolated and do not consider their goals in their mutual interest. In this way, inherent assumptions of authority and power framed by museums have been projecting meanings and stereotypes upon those who are considered "other." Even in the postmodern or multicultural

76

ERY CAMARA (p. 81) was born in Dakar, Senegal, in 1953. He studied visual arts at the National Arts Institute of Dakar. In 1975 he was awarded a fellowship by the Mexican government to study art restoration, receiving an MA at the Manuel del Castillo Negrete National School of Conservation, Restoration and Museography in 1981; three years later, at the same school, he completed an MA in Museum Studies. Camara has continued to live in Mexico City, exhibiting his paintings in solo and group exhibitions, while also working as a museum professional and art critic.

As Deputy Director of Museography at the Museo Nacional de Antropologiá e Historia, Camara organized "El Poder del Sol, Oro de Colombia" (1994). As Deputy Director for Museography and Research at the Museo Nacional de Culturas Populares, he curated "Haiti Chérie, Arte Popular Haitiano" and "Tepito Mito Magico, Albur del Tiempo" and organized "Fiesta de la Muerte" shown at the Musée Botanique, Brussels, as part of "Europalia" (1993). While Deputy Director of the Museo Nacional del Virreinato, Tepotzotlan, he organized "El Mexico Colonial" (1989). Working as an independent curator, Camara organized in 1995 "Echate Ese Trompo a la Uña, Miniaturas Mexicanas" at the Museo Nacional de Culturas Populares and "Altares de Muertos" at the Centro Cultural Bélem, Lisbon; and in 1996 "Instrumentos Europeos de Tortura y de Pena Capital, desde la Edad Media a la Epoca Industrial" at the Centro Cultural de Tijuana.

Camara has presented papers at national and international meetings, addressing issues of multiculturalism, identity, and African contemporary art and society such as the Dakar International Biennial (1992); XXVIII Congress of the International Association of Art Critics, Stockholm (1994); 5th Havanna Biennial, Cuba (1994); 1st Johannesburg Biennial (1995); "Mirarte," Bogota (1996); UNESCO, Paris (1997); and "100 Guests/100 Days" at "Documenta X," Kassel. His writings have appeared in exhibition catalogues most recently, *Face a L'historie* (Centre Pompidou, 1996); *Neue Kunst aus Africa* (Haus der Kulturen der Welt, Berlin, 1996); and *Otro pais, Escalas Africanas Centro Atlantico de Arte Moderno* (Fundacion "La Caixa," 1995). He has also contributed to journals such as *Atlantic International Art Magazine*; *Curare*; *Femam Magazine*; *Images of Africa*; *Metronome*; *Mexico en el tiempo*; and *Poliester Magazine*.

world, the monologue between audience and institution sometimes remains the same. Many people, hypnotized by television and Walkman headphones, sustain the monologue, just as corporations continue their spread of power, ignoring the differences between quantity and quality, dependence and creativity. The standardized behavior and attitudes of passive consumers oppose creativity, which liberates the individual from virtual slavery.

The Reynoldstown neighborhood of Atlanta, a community founded by freed slaves near the railroad, has been a crossroads for many generations and cultures. Today, the principal aim of Reyoldstown is to preserve its history, revitalizing it in new ways while retaining respect for inherent values. During the Centennial Olympic Games this community experienced "Conversations" through creativity, converting waste into works of art. Together we analyzed the impact on Reynoldstown of the Olympic goal of gathering the world in Atlanta.

We questioned, as many people did, how this might bring about changes in the city, especially in the places selected by the organizers and all the others who had an interest in welcoming the world. We compared these venues to locations whose importance was hidden to tourists and the media. The strategies of the state, copied from the advertising industry, clearly encouraged cultural homogeneity and unity. But a cruel and violent event interrupted. Converted into a sensational media event, the bombing of Centennial Park temporarily diminished public attendance at the Olympics. The result was that some favored visits to the High Museum of Art and other cultural events. This bombing, as well as the fire that destroyed the renovation-in-progress at the Margaret Mitchell House on Peachtree Street, made us reconsider the relationship of the public to this event, to public places, and to the representation of a host of issues in public spaces. As virtual conversation, or perhaps exclusion, television was a ticket to the events for whomever could not afford to attend. This conversation we considered virtual, because it offered no immediate interaction, but it was a mediated experience, like so many that dominate our time.

Media converts silence into order on the pretense of not disturbing viewers but actually aims to focus attention for the gain of corporations; little opportunity is given to the audience to say yes or no. Ignorance, a common enemy, grows because television excludes the many points that might enable people to free themselves from exacerbated consumption. The predetermined attitude and the arrogance of those who portray the goals of the collective body for their own gain adds another dimension to the problem. In response, joining with some members of the Reynoldstown community in a series of workshops, we represented in an installation at The Castle the observed contrast between commercial aims and the spirit of fair play, between the projected essence of the Olympic Games and what it represents for our culture, between the local and the global.

Modestly I think that the lived experience in Reynoldstown last summer is more eloquent than whatever can be written, by me or by any other member of the workshop group. Therefore, I believe that it is worth the effort to rethink it and reconsider the overlapped structures that contextualize the artistic expression of *From Monologue to Conversation* and its reception and re-meaning by the audience and community. The curating process brought tools to reshape relations and attitudes facing the integration of contemporary art with cultural policies. The inner aim of this was to achieve a better understanding of the network of realities conditioning our aesthetic values in order to conquer diversity and originality in their endless richness.

Camara

Before January 1996 I had never heard of Reynoldstown. Seventeen years earlier, I had visited Atlanta while accompanying my friend, Mor Thiam, the famous Senegalese drum master. He was touring there with his band Drums of Fire, and he now lives in Atlanta. After several visits and discussions, the Reynoldstown community and its citizens attracted me most. From the outset, I found a shared sympathy woven into the very fabric of our conversations. The community and its citizens have an ongoing project of neighborhood revitalization: restoration of houses, architectural preservation, and creation of spaces for the free expression of community skills. Based within the community center, I found a place where I could share my observations and suggestions.

Coming from a society where values are often very different, I was conscious of my outsider status and sure that the history of American society I had learned about was not born of consensus. Conversing about cultural heritage always brings opportunities for exchange, during which everyone is free to select what is of worth to them and to share mutual interests.

Behaviors transcending historical context enabled us to know how to listen and how to talk, and allowed us to discuss how art practice can benefit a community that takes into its own hands the cultural evolution of its members. It is important to note that the project had to fit our respective interests. My integration into the community linked many of our activities. Daily we became more familiar with each other in the landscape that we explored together in many ways.

I remember during my first conversation with a group of elderly women quilters and ceramicists that they did not feel this project related to them, preferring to push younger generations to assist. This became a way of experimenting with cultural exchange, by structuring links between generations. Mutual respect in this case is not a given; it is a construction through which everyone who is motivated brings to the group an eloquence of aspirations. What remains from these conversations is a memorable relation that converged into a mutual understanding, not previously afforded by other practices. Two persons played important roles of mediation: the director of the Reynoldstown Revitalization Center, Young Hughley, who introduced me to many neighborhood residents in the hope of reviving their passion for artistic expression; and Ben Apfelbaum, who helped me organize much support for the workshop activities.

To respond to the hospitality I received there and to bring more space into our relations, I organized a Senegalese dinner. Around the food, many informal reflections arose about the difficulties of communication, tension in relations with Cabbagetown neighbors, links between beliefs and education, and the continued optimism of the participants in an ongoing community evolutionary process. Catharsis was often part of these debates. The poet Paul Claudel said about food in *l'oeil écoute*:

> Tout repas, en effet par lui même est une communion, sans même que l'intention religieuse à l'état plus ou moins latent existe.... La naïveté et la sincérité en qui les convives autour de la table puisent au même plat et à la même coupe confèrent à cette fraternelle et joyeuse invitation qu'ils s'adressent l'un à l'autre une dignité supérieure à celle d'une réflexion pure et simple.
> (Any meal by itself is communion, regardless of whether or not a more or less latent religious intent exists.... The joyful and brotherly gathering is given a greater dignity than a mere meal by the naïveté and sincerity in which the guests around the table partake of the same dish and the same cup.)

80

Camara

The references for our conversations were many, and our sessions with organizing staff, fellow colleagues, and a diverse group of local professionals gave a particular dimension to this project. The National Black Arts Festival and the Reynoldstown Festival, as well as the Olympics, made a big impact on the cultural life I observed during this period. In particular, the National Black Arts Festival allowed me to see life celebrated by the African-American community. A historic street, Auburn Avenue, was the heart of its market manifestation with its shops, concerts, and museums covering all the cultural interests. Its celebration of the black community is a very complex undertaking that embraces a wide range of aspects of black culture. This gives an opportunity for visitors to establish contacts, admire their diversity, and consume. Referring to visual arts promotion, I felt that it could be interesting to have more information and criticism beyond the simple display of art as an award, as something to sell or to decorate with. Education for the enhancement of the population could also be carried out through lectures and debates with artists and intellectuals. This festival taught me a lot about how African-Americans re-frame what they have inherited from Africa and transcribe it in new attitudes. Obviously many stereotypes have infiltrated so that some people generalize or attempt to rescue art and existence from a frozen concept. Colors, objects, and more documentation of this festival were integrated into different layers of the "Conversations" project.

Even though I was told that the visual arts were not a developed area of local culture, these festival events made me think that undevelopment is a lack of opportunity to benefit from privileges accorded to dominant groups. Individuals who feel a constant lack are more vulnerable to consume whatever is offered. One thing was clear to all the members of the workshop team at Reynoldstown: there was no star system, no genial

Camara

focus; we were just refreshing our relations under new rules built by our predisposition to understand why we are who we assume to be in a social complex.

Our first silences and misunderstandings about concepts like ethnicity, tribal structures, even Africanness and blackness, fused in a new vocabulary of actions and attitudes allowing for dialogue. Focusing on art and culture from our respective points of view, we wanted to give a sense to the space or a space to the sense.

We were not after a legitimization process; our relations were radically sincere, aimed at giving new meanings to old principles and at inventing new forms of subjectivity to disrupt outdated frames and boundaries. This vision gave to our conversations a continuity beyond that time. It was up to everyone to explore it freely. The reintegration back into the community of the work exhibited at The Castle made its nature different from that normally determined by the art market. In the translation of this experience, it is very important to point out that unlike some critics who frame their essays around a process of discovering and launching artists, this was not our aim.

Conversations at Reynoldstown were related to and given new focus by the whole "Conversations" program and the commentaries born from it. Every week we spent two evenings in a relaxed atmosphere. Painting was our basic practice, on pieces of wood we gathered from John Hughley's front yard (pg. 83). We made photographs of the neighborhood and gathered objects that were otherwise destined for the garbage. Verbal interchange, music, jokes, and laughing were part of it. On Saturdays, kids came to my home to paint; on occasion we visited exhibitions as a group, which for many was their first experience in a museum.

Camara

After viewing the exhibition "Souls Grown Deep," for instance, we critiqued the overabundance of objects in so small a space, the discourse of the collector-lender, and the vernacular or exotic frame used in display. We also met one of the artists, Lonnie Holley, who guided us on a visit and gave a workshop. This exhibition motivated the group to comment and react in their own space, widening the experience. On my own I visited many other exhibitions during the Olympics in order to better understand the situation and my interpretations.

This evocation is not a report. It is naturally incomplete without the others' voices, but the news I still receive from those I worked with is satisfying. Out of the time frame of last summer, this process still reaches an unspoken reality that is not seen or focused upon; what really happened cannot be contained by the outlines or theoretical schemes of social scientists.

There is a distance between our representation by those from academic or professional fields and what our presence and presentation properly brought about. The audience had the opportunity to relocate meaning for themselves through the process and to identify distortions provoked by museumification. The installation we created at The Castle showed that the exhibition format was not enough by itself to give a reasonable image or full understanding of the complexity of the project. A catalogue or book can add information for reflection, but the lived experience goes beyond an exhibition. Audiences and even critics fail sometimes in using frames and predetermined assumptions about what they see in the gallery; it is not enough to enable them to receive the subtleties of difference. The display conveys only part of an intangible relationship that remains most vital wherever the participants are rather than in the unavoidably neutralizing museum space.

84

"Conversations at The Castle" was more than an exhibition. Our display confronted many difficulties of the museum and unresolved exhibition issues. Between the coffin, which hung like a cradle, and consumerism anthropomorphized, were wrapped public myths. New expressions of relations convert exchanges into living borders. Like seashores renewing the geometry of limits — displacements of time, people, and objects — the whole iconography of paradoxes brings about more perplexity. The contents of our discussions about media, consumerism, and goals of self-fulfillment were reflected by the network of symbols we used: deserts, migrations, trade, the sane, pictures, sculptures, still life, and "The Rings" exhibition (with its aim of homogenizing passions through world culture under the particular criteria of love, anguish, awe, triumph, and joy), and the television and desk (which critique the autism and voyeurism of technocrats). Maps of categorizations were substituted by stamps, mirrors, money, ladders, eyes, and birds. All these means of correspondence were like messengers to confront those from whom no answer could be received, leading us to wonder seriously whether people really listen to each other, imitating the media in their social relations.

Another question was, is the museum a still life? I remember once I thought that my relation with still life came from offerings where every element acts and plays a particular role; this grew into my reflections about the museum. Why a still life? Both still life and museums are configurations of symbols and space whose significance goes beyond appearance, constructions where time and decomposition can be held or exposed to infinity.

A contrast of textures and approaches originating from different backgrounds structured the questions we raised in our part of the conversations. Our aim was not to encourage consumption but to give people

Camara

space to explore their recreational activities. These conversations showed that there is a lot to do to fight the ignorance and misconceptions fostered by extremist or isolationist attitudes. Sharing the space with the IRWIN installation was very eloquent, pointing to the manipulation of art in the Western world (pp. 78–79). At The Castle the display subverted many stereotypes.

Contrasting with the fetishizing phenomena of the Olympics, "Conversations" got to the depth of some intimacies not found in many institutional spaces. During the Olympics, corporations decorated the city with their advertising. The slogan was "be part of the team." But how? Maybe by homogenizing consumerism to create anonymity in individuals.

Among the Mandingo — my ethnic group — the Jalis and Kora players, who are our living memory, used to illustrate conversations by saying:

> Dunya ning to bala aning kontong'o
> wolong kathiati
> Dunya be mu terkilingneti.
> (If the world has a name and a first name
> it is dialogue.
> The whole world is only one friendship.)

One of the rules of conversation is to know how to listen, to receive from someone what is missing in ourselves or to make a link between our sameness and difference. Listening allows a person to better speak or express him- or herself. But consciousness and cross-cultural exchanges are required within conversations so that there can be different voices, sights, and actions, together with respect among persons. This is to share what it means to be a human or just a being — an energy belonging to the whole — from cave paintings to coffins, from temples, palaces, museums, and malls. To share, to converse, is a part of our search for transcendence, our bridge between death and life, between past, present, and future. It is a constant opposition, and at the same time a transaction, of monologue and conversation, history and memory.

Reynoldstown, Senegal, Mexico, and the whole world provide these questions and answers. In West Africa, we used to say that it is within peace that the whole resides. It is also within peace that the work of art blooms. Here lies a wish that ties us into the spider web in which, according to Bantu philosophy, no fiber can move without making the whole vibrate. Now that the whole world is confronting issues of xenophobia, racism, integrationism, and a new totalitarianism through global marketing, it is worthwhile to recall Fon's wisdom: "For the water in a punctured jar to be saved, all hands need to work together to plug the holes." Art fertilizes human relationships just as water fertilizes the natural world, but let us remark that the exhibition space today is a very sophisticated arena whose power is sometimes conquered by arbitrariness. To create art, face it, and talk about it requires inclusive and progressive attitudes.

As Master Thierno Bokar, the Malian wise man, wrote:

> Whatever the race of man,
> when active contemplation illuminates his soul,
> his soul acquires the brightness of a mystical diamond.
> Neither his color, nor his origin are taken into account.

Camara

does your

society accept you?

We shape our collaborative work around an examination of the components of identity. How do these components form or dis-form (destroy) a personality or a social group? We try not to draw conclusions or point to a single answer but to make visible some of the collective and individual mechanisms at work in a poetical form. Our work is not education, curing, or social service. Art may be all these things, but it is also something broader. We see art as a necessary experience that allows one to feel and use the power of poetry in life, between individuality and society.

We consider interaction to be a form of artistic expression. We base our work in the philosophy that art, as a creative experience, has enormous potential as a communication vehicle among people. We work exclusively through interactive processes in which the representation of themes and issues directly involves concerned people or groups. Our work is not necessarily designed as community-oriented projects but as art realized with communities as part of the larger society, delving into the relationship between these communities and society.

More important than knowing or stating is asking. By exposing fragility or even ignorance we have a possibility of establishing contact with groups of people to which we ourselves do not belong. Influenced by our experience as teachers, we understand that education is a two-way dialogue. Education as interaction is more effective for the development of creativity and thinking. Through exposing our vulnerability, we are able to make genuine contact with others in different situations. For us, art (especially contemporary art), not education, is the best tool for achieving communication and establishing interaction between disconnected territories in society. We work mostly with social groups that are left out of the art world; in this, we have a special interest in youth. Thus, we seek to reaffirm art as a necessary experience outside the political and cultural definitions of society — art as a subversion of culture and politics.

88

MAURICIO DIAS (p. 94) was born in 1964 in Rio de Janeiro where he attended the School of Arts at the Universidade Federal; he completed a specialization degree in Fine Arts at the Schule fur Gestaltung in Basel and emigrated to Switzerland.
WALTER RIEDWEG (p. 91) was born in 1955 in Lucerne, Switzerland and received graduate degrees from the Akademie fur Schul- und Kirchenmusik, Lucerne, and the Scuola Teatro Dimitri in Verscio, Switzerland. Both artists now reside in Basel.

Their first joint work in 1993, entitled *Wanderzeit* (*Times of Migration*), used the medieval Swiss village of Sursee itself as a stage within which the inhabitants — simultaneously performers and audience — reexamined personal stories of having grown up there and projected their memories into the history of the place.

With *Innendienst* (*Inner Service*) in 1995, they brought together 280 immigrant children enrolled in Zurich's "integration school system," through which they are introduced to German. The students were asked to bring jars containing objects and smells, both from their homeland and their new land. Building an associative chain, they arrived at levels of communication that offered insight into the construction of meaning and the relationship of identity and learning a foreign language. An installation of the project at the Shedhalle in Zurich attracted many educators and youth that would not otherwise visit this alternative art space.

Devotionalia (1995–97) was a long-term and multileveled project concerning youth living on the streets of Rio de Janeiro, carried out on site in association with social agencies in Brazil and Switzerland. The youth made wax castings of their own hands and feet from plaster molds in the tradition of the *ex-voto*, a cultural vocabulary familiar to them in its use as a charm to fulfill a desire. Over the three-year period Dias and Riedweg created extensive video documentation of the youths' lives, needs, and dreams. An installation consisting of casts and videos was first exhibited at the Museu de Arte Moderna in Rio in 1996, with subsequent showings in Switzerland, Holland, and Germany. The project concluded in August 1997 with an exhibition at Brazil's National Congress, during which time the artists staged Internet conferences between twenty politicians in Brasilia and twenty favelas and NGOs in Rio. In exchange for donating the installation to Museu de Arte in Brasilia, the Brazilian government established a program to help 100 seventeen-year-olds each year make the transition to independent adulthood.

Question Marks **was primarily an artistic communication process between two groups of people in detention who do not normally have the opportunity to talk and listen to each other. Communication took the form of a video question-and-answer exchange — a conversation — between thirty youth offenders and victims at the Fulton County Child Treatment Center School (FCCTC) and nine prisoners in the Atlanta U.S. Federal Penitentiary (USP).**

In addition to the space that this project afforded for self-reflection and expression of individual and group identities, *Question Marks* became a dialogue that stretched beyond these institutions, giving each group a way to communicate and be heard outside the walls that confine them and to represent themselves as a still extant part of society.

Our primary audience is those who directly participate with us in the process. For *Innendienst* (*Inner Service*, 1995) we spent two months visiting 280 immigrant students in Zurich public schools, then brought them in to make an installation with us at the Shedhalle. For *Devotionalia* (1995–97) we worked with youth on the streets of Rio de Janiero, but unlike the Zurich project, the interaction took place outside of an art space, returning to it later in the form of a display. While we managed to bring in about fifteen hundred people from the streets and favelas to a new territory during the opening at the Museu de Arte Moderna in Rio de Janeiro, in Atlanta we were unable to have the youth we worked with traverse territories, even temporarily. This does not mean that their interaction was any less important, but that their participation had to be conceived with their confinement in mind. Ultimately, the form their interaction took reflected the central theme of the distance between them and society.

In *Question Marks* we continued our research on the components of identity by focusing on prisoners. Criminality and punishment are major issues in the United States today; they make their mark on the country's politics and also contribute to a very specific picture of America in other countries as it is exported in literature, cinema, television, and the visual arts. We came together with a group of people in detention — a pluralistic and nonconclusive panel — to question who is imprisoned, the socio-political circumstances that bring a person to prison, and what confinement provokes in one's identity.

We were attracted to this subject because the Atlanta youths' relationship to crime and the penal system was in many ways similar to that of the youth living on the streets of Rio de Janeiro with whom we had worked in *Devotionalia*. In Brazil, like in many other countries with a history of colonization and slavery, the vast majority of people in detention are black. Like in the United States, about seventy-five percent of the inmate population in Brazil is comprised of black males; in Switzerland, every second inmate is a foreigner. Not only because of our past interests but because of this outrageous reality, we decided to again involve youth in our project in Atlanta. Among the information we initially gathered in January 1996 was a brochure describing a certain boot camp program for youth in detention entitled: "How to de-construct and re-construct a person in ninety days." We were deeply impressed with the manipulation inherent in the use of this sentence as the penal system sought to convince society of its efficiency. By contrast, we consider such a policy to be totally irrational and actually dangerous, above all when it is thought to help youth. This propaganda reminded us more of Nazi methods of exclusion and racial extermination than any real beneficial engagement with youth. Not that we deny the existence of a certain criminal countenance, but it

89

Dias and Riedweg

is extremely important to underscore the fact that at least ninety percent of people in detention are actually products of poverty, left out and unable to participate in the American social system. As one prisoner put it, they are the counter-results of the American dream.

Our references also included *Walls and Bars* by Eugene Victor Debs, written from 1920 to 1923 while inside the Atlanta U.S. Federal Penitentiary; it was published in 1927 after his death. One of the more bizarre chapters of American politics is that Debs ran for president on the Socialist ticket in 1920 while in prison. His book is a portrait of life in prison, in which he makes illuminating points about the structure of the penal system. The reading and debating of his text with the inmates at the USP proved that his commentary is still relevant today.

For us, in order to work in new contexts and make any contribution, we must be conscious of difference and try to promote an exchange of different values. We believe that it was because we were outsiders — foreigners and not part of the penal system, different but respecting difference — that our encounters with people who lived in that system became a fertile field of communication. Even the barriers between us (such as our language difference and different cultural roots) had a positive aspect, because as strangers we were noticed.

This led to communication in situations where discussion had all but evaporated. Because we didn't belong to this place or in this system, all of us — artists, inmates, youth, and staff — had to redefine our roles and find new codes of communication. There was no precedent or pattern of behavior to fall back on. Instead we developed a new form of interaction in which poetry was used as a subversive form of resistance and communication within the system.

90

Much of the nature of our conversations centered on territorial issues. Displacing issues into different territories where they don't usually belong promotes interaction between unspoken or miscommunicated parts. In Rio we could not interact with the issues of street kids without involving the populations of the favelas, social workers of NGOs, the school system, and political authorities. But it is important to displace these different territories to show how they do not work in a coordinated way. This was our aim in displacing the messages of youth and adults incarcerated in Atlanta, in bringing them outside the system in which they are normally seen. In displacing things — and values — art can create a new mix of audience while at the same time enlarging it.

Our framework for conversation was built around eight weeks of workshops at the Fulton County facility and five weeks at the federal prison. These workshops, based on perception exercises, were used to provoke a wider context for discussion and, thus, stimulate a broader range of exchange among the participants. We incorporated some techniques, originally found in therapeutic practices, which we first used as high school teachers in the Swiss public school system. In *Question Marks*, however, these sensory experiences led the participants to discover personal associations from which images were created and to develop interaction as a mode of artistic expression. Through newfound sensitivities and artmaking, an increasing level of dialogue resulted between the two groups of participants.

Dias and Riedweg

Following each workshop, the participants were asked to draw floor plans from memory of the places in their lives: their bedrooms, their homes, their neighborhoods, the court, and their cells (p. 92). They were also asked to place personal things, objects, themselves, or other people — whatever they remembered having — in these drawings. We had never seen these spaces, either because they were from the past or because they were inaccessible, such as their cells, the "houses" they lived in now. (Curiously, while we had an introductory tour around the USP facility, we were never allowed to see beyond the classroom at the FCCTC, although many promises were made. Descriptions of daily life in this facility by staff members and directors were very different from those of the youth.) These drawings became an important means of communication. Each series provided an occasion for discussion on themes of intimacy, behavior, family, childhood, community life, relationships, crime, arrest, sentence, and current situations. These conversations were videotaped and exchanged between the two groups.

With the youth participants we had more time to explore this exchange. Since the places they drew were so different and so important in their lives, this aspect led to the next idea: the making of a nest, a home, a nurturing and secure place. The youth chose to model their nest on those of African weaver birds, who share one nest that has many entrances allowing a multitude of birds to occupy the individual "cells," as they are referred to. The nest the youth created was made by sewing their memories (about 100 acetate strips upon which were written questions from their lives) into a huge amorphous structure of coconut fibers (p. 91). This sculpture eventually found its habitat at The Castle (p. 96).

Dias and Riedweg

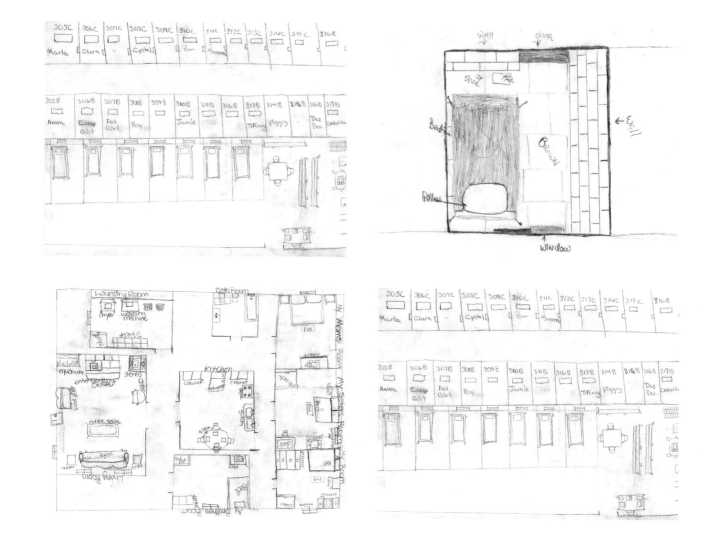

1
"Georgia Correctional Industries, a thirty-six-year old public corporation, makes car license plates, furniture, road signs, and clothes sold to local and state governments. Almost fifteen-hundred inmates assigned to Correctional Industries, which operates in most of the state's prisons, work in exchange with training that could help them get a job. Sales last year totaled some $23.9 million, but if it weren't for the 1997 car license plates, the company would probably be losing money…. Correctional Industries, a money-making arm of the state prison system, spends money freely without documenting it, paid commissions a saleswoman did not earn and suffered mismanagement that would bankrupt a private company, according to an audit." Rhonda Cook, *The Atlanta Journal-Constitution*, June 7, 1996.

License plates became another vehicle for communication since they could transport ideas and make a meaningful link to the primary prison industry and main source of earned revenue.[1] License plates, a prevalent part of our daily lives, are directly tied to those who are removed from everyday society. As a departure on the anonymous inmate-produced plate and also a twist on "vanity plates" as an expression of individuality, we used license plates as a site where youth in detention could speak out in a territory to which they do not have access (p. 95). They asked: Did you put me in to leave me out? Are you who you say you are? Who should I fear? Do you like Newt? Are you lucky? Do you have children? Am I a menace? How would you like to change juveniles? We sought to facilitate an exchange of territories through the exchange of these questions. In three street actions, we gave away 350 of these license plates, affixing them to people's cars and kids' bikes so the questions posed by the youth could move beyond the limits of art and come into circulation on the streets (p. 94).

The impact provoked by *Question Marks* varies according to the interest of each person, but one inmate at USP, Kenny R. (pp. 86–87), perhaps stated it best in our taped interview with him:

> I feel that through this very unique medium of artistic expression … a social perspective is provided on an aspect of society that is both largely ignored as well as misperceived. "Criminals" and/or prisoners are thought to be, it seems, an abstract social entity, separate and apart from society. I feel it is very important that the point be clearly made that prisoners, criminals (juvenile and adult), the undereducated, the underemployed, the homeless, and those who find themselves socially or economically disenfranchised and marginalized in this culture — I feel it is

important that we be perceived in a context other than as statistical data. I think it is important that those marginalized segments of the culture which are just as significant threads in the compositional fabric of this society, have an expressive medium to articulate their aspirations and fears, moments of joy and pain, their heartfelt memories, and idealized hopes for the future. I would hope that through participation in this artistic endeavor, we have expressed the inescapable fact that, most of all, we, too, are members of the human family, in spite of our apparent flaws and perceived foibles. I strongly feel this project will do much to "humanize" the perception of statistical/stigmatized entities such as myself.

We also made two companion installations at The Castle. The public — both inside and outside — was present in our thinking from the beginning. The public is basic to our understanding of contemporary art. Yet as in any exhibition, really, the visitor audience is not specific, not visibly known ahead of time. We did not know who our audience would be at The Castle in the same way we did at the two institutions in which we worked. But we endeavored to make a presentation that could be open to others and be part of another territory, the realm of the so-called general public, paradoxically both anonymous and real. Because the subject of prisons is one in which we all have a place — inside or outside — we thought this might allow for larger participation, even interaction, around the attitudes we hold toward those contained there, especially youth. How this broader audience would perceive our project depended not only on the project itself but also on how the audience, exposed to the violence of American media and right-wing politics, subscribed to a belief in the existence of the criminal countenance.

Dias and Riedweg

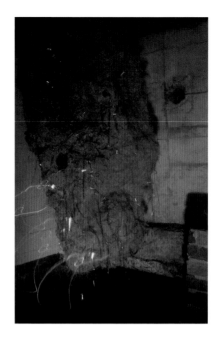

96

In one installation, we projected onto the wall a video based on the interaction that had taken place. On the two levels of floor that lay in front, we projected slides: large, carpet-like images of the license plates, alternating them with those of floor-plan drawings. By walking on and in the spaces drawn by the participants, viewers became part of a kind of virtual environment. In this same area, overlaying the projections, some of the "Conversations on Culture" took place; exhibition space, with its virtual overtones, gave way to actual, interactive discussion space.

This installation was also situated adjacent to The Castle's public Internet center, which we incorporated, too, with the use of our home page. Above the line of computers, through a "slot" in the wall, visitors saw flashing images, beckoning them to enter through the door at the far end of the wall. Here a second installation was constructed around the idea of virtual isolation. The slide projection, previously visible only in part through the slot, now covered the entire interior wall. This wall had a slot, too, and viewers were positioned in the narrow dark space between these parallel outside and inside slots. Inspired by the architecture of the space (a kind of old kitchen with a brick fireplace and no window), we decided to seal off the room, creating a kind of cell. Inside was the nest made by the youth at the FCCTC (p. 96); it filled the space, hanging from the ceiling to just above a water-flooded floor. As viewers approached the slot (p. 97), they could hear parts of taped conversations among the youth while working on the nest. Shifting uncomfortably to reposition one's sight line and take in the whole, viewers could at best catch glimpses of the nest through the slot. Its full image existed only in reflection — in the water or in the slides on the outer wall where the questions embedded in the nest became visible. Thus, the experience of the sculpture became more virtual

Dias and Riedweg

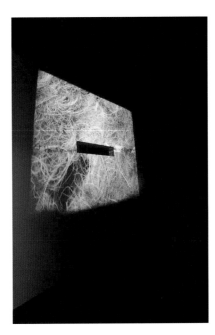

We would like to thank those individuals who, in addition to our dedicated assistant Gabriela Fitz, helped shape the entire project through their active participation: Nasheema, Joe, Shekeytta, Dirk, Matthew, Sophie, Yanita, Darius, Daniel, Daniel G., Germaine, Maurice, Carla, Erica, James, Jamie, Tiffany, Melvin, Shedria, Chaka, and others among the 130 youth at the FCCTC during the Olympic summer of 1996; and Kenny, Joe, Donald, Brian, Abelardo, Hector, Daniel, Toni, and Jimmy at the USP. In the negotiations with the institutions, we received support from Dr. Richard Ellis, head of the psychology department at USP; Susan Bishop, chaplain at Metro Correctional Institution, a women's prison in Atlanta; Karen Galvin and Almo Carter of the Office of Programs and Development at Fulton County Juvenile Court; and Dr. Carrie Roseberry, principal of the public school within FCCTC. Ginger Lyon, Cathy Hudson, and LaVone Griffin and Rebecca Ranson (both of whom are artists who have worked on cultural projects in Atlanta prisons) also contributed to the development of our project.

than actual. The impossibility of seeing the whole nest, as well as the sensation of standing in an "in-between space" from where one saw slices of other spaces evoked the distance that exists between society and prison.

It was in a space in between the virtual and actual existence of those confined that we worked as artists in *Question Marks*. Yet we missed being able to build a stronger communication between the inmate-participants and the general audience. Time was too short for us to explore all the possibilities that developed. For instance, we could not involve the institutional staff members who over time became more interested and receptive. But for that reason, we initiated contacts with institutions in Atlanta to try to find ways that this project or a version of it could continue. Nonetheless, even within the time frame in which it existed, we believe *Question Marks* achieved many of its goals and opened up a surprising space for interaction. Conversations were provoked, which was the goal.

We did not and do not control the effects of these conversations. Art differs from social service, education, healing, and other functions exactly because it is not conceived to control or produce a certain outcome. We don't expect it will change the things we don't agree with, but we do believe and hope it can have a place in that change, having contributed different points of view and, perhaps, shown some other possibilities.

Dias and Riedweg

Brothers For Others: Sports, Surrogacy, and Society

My approach to my emerging practice has been one of continual investigation and questioning, mostly for my own understanding of the environment in which I might temporarily find myself upon taking up an invitation to do a work. In fact, a continual reexamination of my role as an artist has become a way of living and working, as I am constantly moving through new territories. Most sites are unfamiliar, and each is dramatically different.

Usually there are expectations as to how I might behave or function as an artist. From the outset I have been curious about those expectations or behavior models. By "behavior" I mean traditional role playing according to definitions of "artist" and, more specifically, the aesthetic, public, and social functions the artist is to assume. My curiosity came about by default. I became wary of being useful in a traditional mode, but I had no other immediate answer as to how I might function. So I went looking for a job.

I became interested in finding places in which the artist can work, places that through history, politics, and social circumstances have excluded the artist from being active. There I perceived a role for the artist, not as social worker, but as something else. By means of immersion and exploration, I felt the artist could find a place. I believe it is unhealthy for the artist to work in isolation, and if the artist is to become more engaged with the world, then the nature of that engagement should be a subject for discussion — and could be the art itself.

In the case of Atlanta, it was necessary to develop a way to present myself and what I might "do" in a concrete manner. This served as a basis for gaining trust and access. My approach, as in times before, was one of integration: to become part of a cultural and social structure and to try to understand how it functions. This does not mean I identify with that structure or that I become assimilated into it. Rather, being an outsider allows a certain freedom to explore and to reveal certain aspects of the community. This informs my practice as it becomes a way of locating or speculating on a possible function for me as an artist.

MAURICE O'CONNELL (pp. 98–99) was born in 1966 in Dublin where he still resides. He studied there at the National College of Art and Design, receiving his BA in fine art in 1992. Since that time he has worked inside and outside of institutions, using exhibitions, installations, education programs, residencies, and public commissions to address how people who do not usually look at art encounter and perceive culture. He constructs site-related situations around his own public presence that allow for interactions and in-depth engagement with others. He explores alternative ways in which the artist can work and identifies different routes by which the audience can be involved in that work, while probing the role of the artist in society today and the artist's relationship to the audience.

O'Connell's most extensive project to date as an artist-organizer-educator has been *Tribal Field* (1993-95) aimed to counteract the ineffectualness of community centers in densely populated areas of Dublin. Over three consecutive summers he brought together 1,500 students in a large abandoned field in the vicinity of the Irish Museum of Modern Art (IMMA), entering into simultaneous conversations with the museum, the community, and the government regarding the role of art education and the welfare of youth. Using games as a means of socialization and learning, *Tribal Field* enabled artists and students to work together around themes of territory, identity, and journey; inhabitation; and finally personal mark making. In 1995 he also undertook *Role Response Research* as part of the exhibition "From Beyond the Pale" at IMMA in which he remained confined in a room in the museum, twenty-four hours a day for one month, depending upon the staff and visitors to provide for his care and communicating to them only through gestures.

As part of the 1996 exhibition "Manifesta" at the Boijmans Van Beuningen in Rotterdam, O'Connell's project *Institutional Relations* examined the relationship of staff and visitors to the building and functions of the museum in order to understand the institution's cultural intentions. The artist's interest has focused on developing user strategies at arts institutions, taking the stance that the audience has a potential role within cultural production and the understanding of culture. *Live/Life from Within* (1997) at the Barbican Centre, London, was directed toward solving problems related to existing audiences. Continuing his role of artist-as-consultant in an ongoing series of projects, "Can We Talk! We Need to Talk!," he is working at the IKON Gallery, Birmingham, England, on an initiative to engage new audiences.

Working with children in Ireland, the United Kingdom, and Europe, I have seen how their lives have become increasingly difficult and their environments more hostile. As family circumstances deteriorate and communities come under threat, I have felt compelled as an artist to become involved in lobbying, advocacy, and the development of education programs based on art. My work is critical in nature out of a necessity to address the circumstances in which increasing numbers of people find themselves. The circumstances of children are not geographically specific.

While in the past my practice has involved children and brokered ways in which they and I could be engaged with each other, in Atlanta — for the first time — I was provided with an opportunity to explore those parties who mediate my work and who, at the same time, are the parties that mediate these children's lives. **This was an opportunity to understand the complex layers of relationships involved in cultural practice outside the art system, which, ultimately, involve me. While previously I had developed models by which I could engage others in order to fulfill a community function, in Atlanta I sought to apply a model by which the engagement itself was the "work." That is, I sought to use the possibilities here to examine the nature of engagement, the relationships and ramifications between persons inside and outside the art system.**

In this approach my aspirations were open-ended; I was not sure what I might find, and halfway through I was overwhelmed by all I was seeing. But as I moved through the structures, it was possible to develop a thesis; I was not looking for it per se, but it evolved. My plan was to enter this unfamiliar territory, try to understand in some way its nature and relationship to the larger social structure, and then, as an artist, explore how appropriate I might be to that environment. My four-month relationship with Atlanta and with some of its inhabitants included long hot afternoons watching children and adults; early morning critical-theory breakfasts; conversations with directors of charity funding agencies, often with them requesting further meetings; dialogue and disagreement with the other participating artists; three-hour back-to-back conversations with visitors to The Castle who were encountering my practice and challenging it. The main element was a form of engagement as art based on the artist's — my — presence. Some of what I initially proposed did not take place, but much more than I expected ended up occurring. The more I engaged, the deeper the involvement became, having originally held out little promise other than the encounter.

I explored what I called the "service provision" for children and how I fit into it. This originally stemmed from a question I had asked at a conference in 1994 of some of the world's leading cultural funding agencies: Why use youth to achieve their cultural aims and ambitions? I asked this repeatedly, but there was no response. To me, the irony of this lay in the fact that the title of the conference was "Youth, Culture, and Europe." In Atlanta there were numerous answers in the many cultural programs of the Boys & Girls Clubs and other social agencies. Still the questions were there, too: Why art, why artists, why children?

By breaking down the project into three phases, I established various points of dialogue with different constituents at The Jesse Draper Boys & Girls Club, one of fifteen clubs in Atlanta, at the Clubs' administrative offices, and at The Castle. First, I spent six weeks at the Boys & Girls Club, becoming a regular among the children and staff. I used this environment to explore and not necessarily be useful. This lack of working on something caused some confusion at the outset, but as we continued not to work together, the situation relaxed; I was an artist, not *the* artist. I was asking questions and rarely answering them. Artists not having the answers but rather looking for them in those persons the artist engages became an interesting position. Here I was presenting myself as willing to engage and learn. Interestingly, there seemed to be no limit to the questions and people who could be engaged. On many occasions I did not agree with all I encountered, but I was informed through this process of exposure. At the Draper Club I tried to understand the relationship of the child to the adults whose job it was to take care of them. Over time it was possible to ask questions about broader aspects of the children's lives and the society in which they exist.

In the second phase, located in the executive offices of the Boys & Girls Clubs of Metro Atlanta and its parent organization, the United Way, I searched deeper into what such service providers offer children and their communities, gaining some sense of the larger scope of these organizations and the surrogate relationships they have developed. I spoke with staff about their jobs and their understanding of the role they play in the lives of children at the Boys & Girls Clubs. I met with those in positions of responsibility, who affect the outcome of these children's lives. In my discussions I tried to understand how this structure had come into place, how it was functioning, and its implications for the future of communitie — communities that in past projects I would have engaged and worked with directly and constructively.

The conversations that took place were about the city and a part of its population, about people's hopes and fears for themselves and for others, and about the people who made it their business to do something to ensure children's lives, turning that task into a business.

From these dialogues was drawn a picture of a highly complex organizational structure that had developed and was replacing an already dysfunctional model. Repeatedly, agencies identified home and community as lacking in essential elements needed to nurture a child's future. This role is not new, but what may be different is the extent and scale of this practice today. It seemed these agencies were essential to and responsible for determining the child's future. My conversations also dealt with why and with what understanding these persons became so enthusiastic about my previous modes of work, and with their belief that art could help them in their work. In Atlanta there was continuous local broadcast of care and concern for the city's children, with an apparent relationship to art. Curiously this was set against the backdrop of the other major cultural exhibitions and performances presented during the Olympics.

The assumption that art can work for everyone is a difficult one. One must ask what purpose art serves. Whose purpose does it serve? How can it serve this purpose? I sought to investigate others' motivations to use art in a social sphere, to explore parallel aspects between, say, the needs of youth-at-risk and contemporary art, particularly through the strategic forms of public or community-based art practice. Why art? Why artists?

In a strange sense, as I continued my search for a role or function for art and the artist, I was continuously faced with numerous examples that offered as their premise the artist's social role in benefiting kids' lives. Many of the sites I encountered, in fact, were all but inundated with cultural activity to the point of complacency. This made me wary and critical of existing practice and models of community art. I began to see gaps of understanding in others' as well as my own practice regarding artists' roles if they are not of that community; their long-term responsibility and accountability; their work in the cultural realm for purposes other than purely aesthetic ones; ethics; and the danger of a colonial hybrid as some artists enter new domains ill-informed and motivated in ways that might be unhealthy. I say this not only based on artist- or agency-initiated projects, but also similar interventions made by the private sector (commerce-as-culture) that without too much squinting of the eyes shift into art interventions. Art's commercial application was much heightened and showcased during the Olympics with Coca-Cola's "Coca-Cola Kids" and "Paint Pals"; Nike's "Images of Excellence"; Fuji's "Photo Pals"; and Visa's "Olympics of the Imagination," all of which tied together service, children, art, and cultural exchange.

In the end, perhaps ironically, I made nothing with the people I met. We did not work together. I was permitted to enter their lives, to watch and journey with them throughout the summer. But as the process of investigation wore on, an ever-present dilemma reemerged. Tradition muscled in, demanding overtly or implicitly that we produce, showcase, and (of particular concern to me) represent. In my practice I hope to relieve art from the obligations of representation. My work has qualitive concerns but not artistic aspirations (as in a display of talent). Thus, I tried as much as possible to present and not represent. This has obvious problems fitting into traditional or current modes of artmaking. Even among those engaged in the process, there were confusions over art production and representation. Having listened, some still felt uncomfortable with the notion that art exists only in this form of discussion. The quiet hope remained that something of that experience might be represented instead of just allowed to unfold. In other words, my approach felt to them like a denial of the vicarious experience as it might exist in a photographic record of the children and me meeting them. This is a common thread that runs through community-based projects; for me, that form of witnessing is not possible.

What is interesting to me is the dilemma of exclusion-inclusion and where I, the artist, meet the public or publics. For me, public art is limited to particular publics, and accessibility is limited through participation. This does not mean I am limiting involvement, but rather that I am not subscribing to a "publicness" of art achieved through inherently claimed universality, a traditionally postured global appeal. I suppose I find the notion of audience in traditional terms redundant; the audience is already there, integrated into the process. My work becomes public because of its very specificity and depth of individual engagement. The type of person I engage becomes restricted or limited by the places where I am present.

For this reason, in Atlanta I moved to different sites and locations, engaging others and getting more answers. Finally, my audience in Atlanta became those who participated in the experience. So in a sense my populist approach becomes avant-garde as public art becomes private. Whether it is taken in as a personal-public experience depends on what motivations are supplied to the audience and what interests the individual has in being engaged in the particular subject. The author of the experience, the artist — me — is not anonymous but also not necessarily as central as in modernist and, frequently, postmodernist practice. My work has tried to locate the artist in these multiple worlds. I do not bring my world to others as a means of influence or, as some might claim, to save lives and communities. I do not position myself in the central role, therefore implying a dependency. Rather the relationship is "democratic." I am not in a position to say how the experience may have affected others, nor even how they define it. I see this not as a collective experience but as multiple experiences with different values placed on what happened. There is not the referential object to return to, just people's definition or interpretation of their part in the experience. The legacy of this kind of work is its lack of colonialism; its resonance is in the interpretation of experiences, not in a dependency on those experiences. There is self-interest, but it is rarely exploitive. This understanding helps the artist keep the conversation going without being irresponsible.

O'Connell

So to deal with this desire for something tangible (which even I felt), I introduced display components in the last phase of the project: an installation entitled *Who Cares* at the Youth Art Connection Gallery/Boys & Girls Clubs of Metro Atlanta (pp. 106–107) and an office at The Castle. Surprisingly, the Internet also became a useful research tool and dialogue facilitator.

I did not see the display components as my culminating product or "art" but rather as just that: components. They were part of my research as presentation elements, but the research itself was in fact the core of the art. These components were used to motivate other people who were outside the earlier phases of the process, to engage and to ground them in a shared discussion.

The Youth Art Connection Gallery is shared with the downtown headquarters of the Boys & Girls Clubs and United Way, where I had spent weeks speaking with the staff. The social service sector's newly asserted union with art is represented here by its own dedicated exhibition and workshop space. I presented a composite collage of snapshots I took of kids at the Draper Club (p. 104); a wall of slogans — real and fictitious — of service programs for kids; and a series of display cases with bits and pieces, mementos and trophies I had accumulated over the summer, residue of Olympic-spirited programs for the "benefit" of kids.

At The Castle, I set up an office, reclaiming a makeshift basement living space complete with sink, to which I added a desk, telephone, computer with Internet access, elements from my summer research, and chairs for visitors (pp. 98–99). It took its inspiration from the "memorial office" of patron Jesse Draper installed at the entrance to the Draper Boys & Girls Club (p. 105), a condensed composite of Mr. Draper's

O'Connell

own office during his lifetime. It is a kind of mausoleum, a vestige of the white benefactor's actual entrepreneurial career that seems oddly foreign to the poor, primarily black kids served by the club. My functional office of a ficticious agency based at The Castle — Brothers for Others (BFO) — was a place from
which I engaged people in an evolving conversation on the possible ways that art and the artist can engage
a society. It was not a set piece or performance, as some observers mistakenly assumed, but a fluid, living,
actual activity.

In its three phases, this work presented an approach to how an artist might exist in the public realm while
not serving traditional expectations. I believe I revealed aspects about the lives of children and those who
manage those lives, and revealed problems and difficulties within the realm of community-based public
art — its long-term responsibility and accountability. The conceptual friction of an artist doing "nothing"
and the need for authored products and representation caused tension among many. To me the project's
success was that it happened outside of traditional modes of art practice, taking the form of discussion
and challenging our understanding of current modes of art practice, art production, and the representation of that production as practice.

**"Conversations" was a testing ground for a developing awareness of my and others' cultural practice. It was an
opportunity to demystify community-based art forms in a forum that is not often made available. To me, it
was important to examine artistic practice — to have a conversation on the subject — because it is important today
for artists to find new ways of working with integrity and clarity of purpose.**

O'Connell

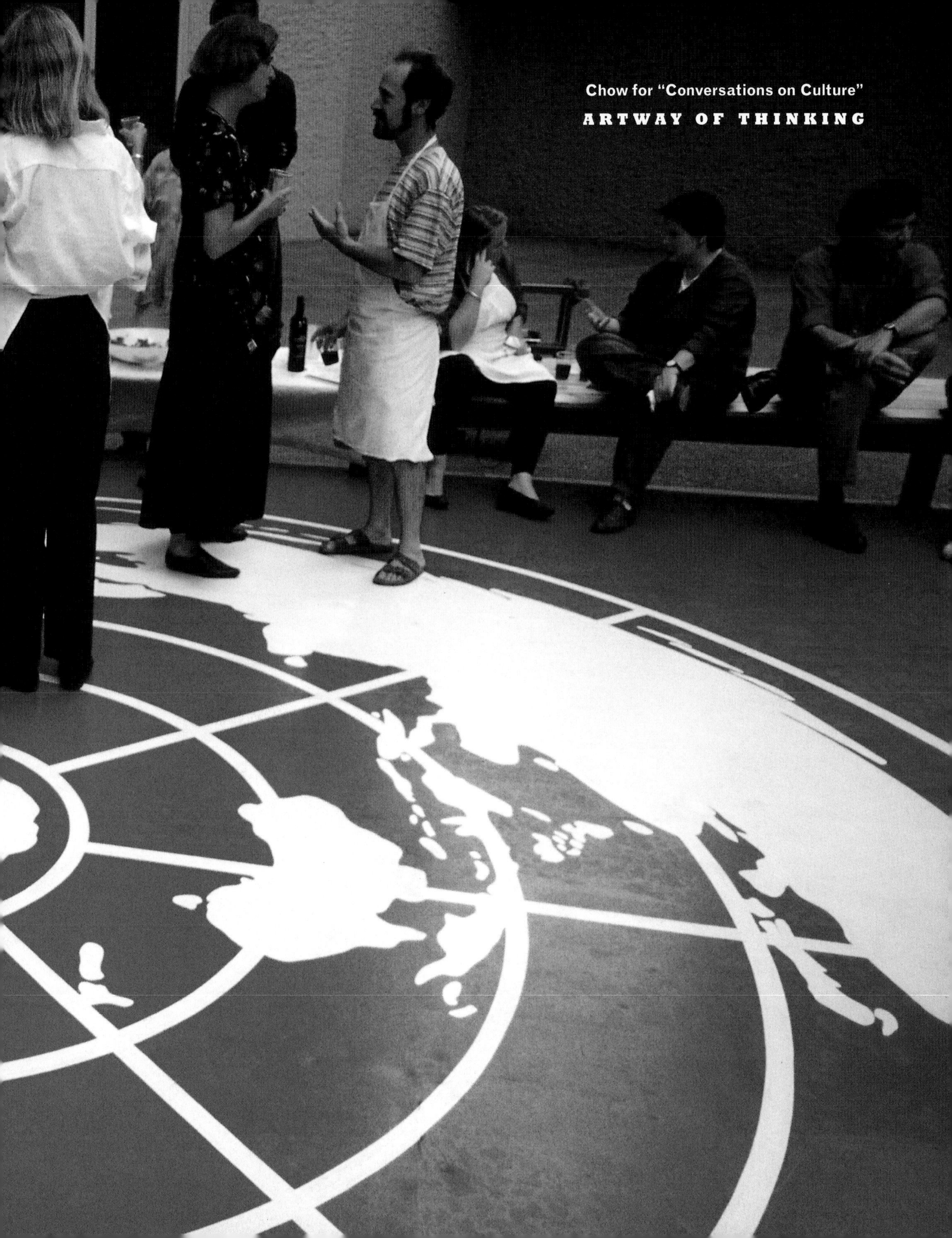

Chow for "Conversations on Culture"

ARTWAY OF THINKING

Food has an exceptional ability to speak about culture, individual identity, and integration. It is a way by which we can open ourselves to other cultures and identities without traveling away from home. It can become a common language for creating a dialogue among different people and cultures. The concept of our project was developed around the medium of food, which we sought to use to facilitate an intercultural and interdisciplinary exchange.

Chow sought to transform the seven roundtable discussions in "Conversations on Culture" into *convivi*-dinners, gatherings during which persons from different places and professions could come together to share ideas and a meal. The menu and method of food preparation, as well as the location of each dinner, was determined in relation to the topic. Through these different ways of coming together, we hoped to stimulate communication and self-expression, giving and receiving, tasting and listening, savoring difference.

In *Chow* we intended to activate a dynamic system of exchange that, for us, has roots in the reality of everyday life and in our Italian culture. In Italy the meal is a way of making guests comfortable and honoring their presence. All important conversations happen around the dinner table; they are hard to forget, as the memory of a conversation expands with the flavor and smell of the food, with the colors of the table. Moreover, as Italians we believe that meals are catalyzing elements that lead people to open themselves to others. We can speak about ourselves over a meal. We hoped food would help the Atlanta guests in their dialogues about art and culture. Thus, in *Chow* we focused on food and the table as a means of welcoming and sharing, as an expression of creativity and self-communication, and as a gift of our time and ourselves to others.

In English, chow is slang for food and is used to express the action of eating (to chow down). The word comes from the Mandarin Chinese *chao* (to stir-fry). The coincidence of the Italian greeting *ciao* (pronounced the same) with this English-Chinese hybrid, made it a perfect international title for our welcoming gatherings. *Chow* evoked the international and cross-cultural dimension we hoped to create.

ARTWAY OF THINKING (p. 112) is the collaborative team of Federica Thiene (born in Vicenza, 1965) and Stefania Mantovani (born in Treviso, 1966) Both attended the Accademia di Belle Arti in Venice, receiving their BAs in 1989 and 1991, respectively. Thiene went on to the University of California at Santa Barbara, completing a MFA in 1990; Mantovani pursued work in architecture, design, and theater.

In 1991 they set up *Progetto Cuspide*, an educational and research program with American and Italian universities in which students found spaces and developed collaborative projects with persons inside urban and social structures. Beginning in 1992, they created *Ad Hoc*, a series of propositions on new uses for the Venice Biennial spaces. By 1993 Thiene and Mantovani formally took on the identity of artway of thinking, an association conceived as an interdisciplinary and intercultural force, its plural identity changing in correspondence to context and the specific problems and circumstances of a situation. As participatory and collaborative undertakings, artway of thinking traverses art, culture, society, and the urban and natural environment. For their part in the 1994 exhibition "soggetto Soggetto," in collaboration with the Museo d'Arte Contemporanea Castello di Rivoli, artway realized *Zona-Riuso*, a project on recycling. While in the gallery they used materials from industry and leftovers from the other artists in the show, in its larger structure this work amplified the "function" of the museum by bringing the museum together with the Comune di Rivoli, Associazione Industriali di Milano, the furniture manufacturer De Rosso Arredamenti, and the local school system to work collaboratively on new cultural strategies for the city. Seeking to employ financial systems alternative to the art market, artway initiated *Box-Culture* in 1995. This ongoing collaborative project with the artists' space Viafarini, Milan, is an Internet data bank of art opportunities and international funding sources along with an on-line consulting service. Commissioned by the European Community, they began in 1994 to develop interdisciplinary strategies for improving the natural and cultural quality of life in Dortmund, Germany, in *Lebensmittel-Approvvigionamenti*. In 1997 their socio-cultural plan for the area of "Colli Berici" around Vicenza was funded under the Leader II program of the European Community. It was developed with I Habitat, an interdisciplinary research group comprised of artists, architects, biologists, and other technicians with whom artway began to work in 1994 on the development of ecological and economical environments. The investigations of artway of thinking continue; in 1997 they proposed two projects for sustainable urban systems for the cities of Fidenza and Salsomaggiore in collaboration with G8 Architectural Associates.

Food, more than any other medium, simultaneously speaks specific and universal languages. It carries its culture as it moves through the market and goes into other cultures. It can retain its identity elsewhere, or even be the location of that identity in a foreign place; like peoples and cultures it can change and become something else through a process of exchange over time and place.

With this intervention we sought to create spaces for interaction. Art must have "trans-" and "inter-" dimensions; there we can establish relationships and affiliations. It is in such interdisciplinary and international spaces that art today finds its identity and purpose.

We depart from the traditional places for displaying art, places considered sacred and that lead one to think that art is realizable only in these locations. In *Chow* **we sought to find a space in which we as artists could speak, communicate, and at the same time listen; people could create an exchange, an interaction, a "conversation."**

In our culture *conversazione* is a word that means a friendly way to talk, to compare, to be open, to listen, to have an exchange. It supposes a condition not always confidential but cozy and close, where time moves slowly and everybody feels comfortable.

With *Chow* we chose not to speak directly to the public but to construct a conversation among those working to broaden the place of contemporary art in the public sphere of culture. To be sufficiently intimate and constructive, these conversations became, in essence, private conversations on public issues. Within a public program like "Conversations at The Castle," this paradox caused some consternation from outside. As with community-based art, which usually involves a specific constituent public, the dinner guests were our community. On the other hand, we also wanted to expand the dialogue; thus we added a dimension to our conversations that continues still today, that is, on the Internet.

111

Our art often seeks to blur the borders between insiders (the art world) and outsiders (society), working in and with society. We feel that this is the only meaningful way to work as artists today. In art that assumes a form approaching life, everyone participates in the artistic moment.

But this is not the same as saying that a single art project can communicate to all people; no single artistic event can meaningfully reach everyone equally. However, a single project can define its boundaries and in doing so move beyond conventional territories and definitions of audience. As artists, we feel a responsibility to change the insider-outsider paradigm in art. Thus, we seek to address two audiences: first the public located in society and then the public located in the art world.

Collaboration, the coming together as family, is a key strategy we employ for bringing others into art. Participation is experience, absorption, and involvement in a system of relations in a place between reality and representation. Collaboration means not only bringing your resources to the situation but also working, giving, and receiving in the situation through a dynamic dialogue, creating a work that is more than one alone could achieve. Sharing an artistic evolution, we bring together individual talents for a common goal, integrating and enlarging the project's possibilities. For example, in *Chow* we found a great collaborator in Massimo Frigatti (pg. 112); he brought to this project his technical skill and culinary art. Thus, a chef entered the art world and we, as artists, entered the kitchen — each with the idea of communicating through food.

artway of thinking

We undertook numerous collaborations with Italian artisan industries and food companies: Illy Caffè, Nino Franco Spumanti, de Majo/ Vetreria in Murano (p. 30), and Az. Vinicola Pagotto. We also collaborated with Kirsten Evans at Blink Multimedia Design in Atlanta to create an extensive website. Moreover, we contacted sixteen people who we deemed to have made significant changes in Italian cultural, social, and political life through their work and asked them to participate by lending us a plate from their own homes. Surprisingly, this initiated our first "conversations," as these persons (only a few of whom we had known before) invited us to their kitchens to talk about and select the plate, so earnestly was this proposition embraced. In Atlanta, as the guests selected their positions at the table, so too did they choose their plates and symbolic "partners." In Italy these individuals could follow the discussions on the Internet. Thus, the sixteen plates expanded the debate beyond Atlanta and the two weeks over which these dinners took place.

Chow was intended to interact, converse, and mingle with another dimension: to fuse life ("Conversations on Culture") with art (Chow) and make them one. It proved a challenging integration, yet when Chow and "Conversations" were together, a greater energy was created. Those involved seemed to realize how art can aid communication and to understand our vision of an art so close to life that anybody can become a part of it. Working inside another structure (a curatorial and critical program) demanded flexibility as changes and influences modified the form of the art and the program. As artists, we had to rethink our claims to "property" (the definition of our work and of art). For instance, although we wanted to create a familiarity among the guests, we ourselves were guests in different facilities,

without the time to develop deep collaborative relationships with those working there. Thus, it became logistically difficult to transform these institutional sites and give them the warmth and atmosphere of a kitchen. The problem of time, shifting guest lists, and the reality of the Atlanta food market kept the project in an ongoing state of development.

An art that operates in and with life is based on compromise; reciprocal concessions happen in the process of development and making, hopefully in a creative and innovative mode. Like culture, which itself is complex and diffuse, the process of carrying out a project that joins art and life is a negotiation more than a controlled process.

This project has led us to contemplate the nature of interaction and creativity. What and how much can we anticipate and resolve during planning in order for a project to succeed? To what extent can we modify our ideas according to the real circumstances that we encounter during the process? What are the dynamics and results of collaboration? Where are the limits on creative property, and which decisions are artistic ones? How can a project be most effective when undertaken in another country, in a different culture with a different point of view in interpreting our message and the structure of our project? *Chow* has been an important step in our research on producing art as a project-in-progress.

LUTTHER BLISSET (Bologna)
is an ever-expanding collective that
anyone can join by using this anonymous but
recognized appellation to "sign" artistic
or social protests, actions, or events.

August 18
TOM ECCLES
Public Art Fund, New York

August 19
VINCE ANTHONY
Center for Puppetry Arts, Atlanta

August 24
GAIL KING GRIFFIN
teacher, Atlanta

August 25
SYLVIA JONES
youth participant, Atlanta

KAREN LUIK
High Museum of Art, Atlanta

PAMELA D. SEZGIN
Teaching Museum South, Fulton County Schools, Atlanta

FELICIA TAYLOR
College Bound Program, Boys & Girls Clubs of Metro Atlanta

August 28
MONIQUE CURNEN
Arts Festival of Atlanta

SUSAN KRANE
University of Colorado Art Galleries, Boulder

August 30
REBECCA DES MARAIS
Youth Art Connection Gallery/Boys & Girls Clubs of Metro Atlanta

CATHERINE FOX
The Atlanta Journal-Constitution

PAT FULLER
public art consultant, Boston

WALTER RIEDWEG
artist, Basel

ANN TEMKIN
Philadelphia Museum of Art

MAURIZIO CATTELAN (Milan) is a conceptual artist who
works within the established gallery system while also challenging and
extending its boundaries through his provocative actions and installations.

August 19
DOUG ASHFORD
artist, New York

August 20
EDA CUFER
critic, Ljubljana

August 24
GWENDOLYN DRISCOLL
CARE World Headquarters, Atlanta

August 25
MELANIE FERNANDEZ
Ontario Arts Council, Toronto

August 28
REGINA FRANK
artist, Berlin

August 30
JAMES MEYER
Emory University, Atlanta

ALLE BARETTINE (Trieste) is a
restaurant employing the disabled that
was established by Impresa Sociale in the 1980s
when funding for psychiatric hospitals
was eliminated under Italy's Basaglia Laws.

August 20
JEFFREY BABCOCK
Cultural Olympiad, Atlanta

August 24
WALTER RIEDWEG
artisti, Basel

August 25
AMINA DICKERSON
Corporate Contributions, Kraft Foods Foundation, Chicago

August 28
LISA TUTTLE
Arts Festival of Atlanta

August 30
FEDERICA THIENE
artist, Venice

SUSY BLADY & PATRIZIO ROVERSI
(Bologna) are television authors and hosts who
bring banal, everyday occurrences to the usually
glamorous TV screen and have set off an
aesthetic revolution in the media.

August 19
MICHAEL DOBBINS
Department of City Planning, Atlanta

August 20
DANIEL MARTINEZ
artist, Los Angeles

August 24
LAVONE GRIFFIN
Theatrical Visionaries, Atlanta

JEFFREY KASTNER
ArtNews, New York

August 25
LINDA BURNHAM
High Performance, North Carolina

JENNIFER FRIDAY
Centers for Disease Control, Atlanta

August 28
DARRYL MAPP
youth participant, Atlanta

August 30
STEFANIA MANTOVANI
artist, Venice

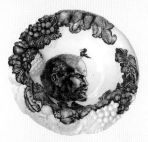

GIANCARLO POLITI (Milan) is editor of
Flash Art, president of *Flash Art* Trevi Museum, and an art
critic whose ideas have evolved with changes in the definition
of art and modes of cultural production over the decades.

August 20
IVAN KARP
Emory University, Atlanta

August 24
MICHAEL BRENSON
critic, New York

August 25
TORREON THOMPSON
youth participant, Atlanta

August 28
ARTURO LINDSAY
Spelman College, Atlanta

August 30
MAURICE O'CONNELL
artist, Dublin

STEFANO BENNI
(Bologna) is a novelist who
transforms, with humor and satire, the
absurdities and banalities of everyday existence
in order to heighten our conscious
perception of contemporary life and
lend to it greater meaning.

August 18
PEARL CLEAGE
West End Performing Arts Center, Atlanta

August 19
NED RIFKIN
High Museum of Art, Atlanta

August 20
CAROL BECKER
The School of the Art Institute of Chicago

August 24
TRICIA WARD
ARTScorpsLA, Los Angeles

August 25
CHARLES SESSOMS
artist, Atlanta

August 28
KAREN LEAGUE
Board of Directors, Arts Festival of Atlanta

August 30
RON PLATT
Southeastern Center for Contemporary Art, Winston-Salem

SERENA DANDINI (Rome) is a
television author and host who employs parody in
her programs for Italian public station RAI 3
to make current critical issues accessible and
to bring them into the popular discourse.

August 18
MAIKA POLLACK
Parkett, New York

August 20
GARY SANGSTER
Contemporary Museum, Baltimore

August 24
DAVID LEVI-STRAUSS
critic, New York

August 25
MAUREEN SHERLOCK
critic, Chicago

August 28
ADRIAN KING
Corporate Contributions, The Coca-Cola Company, Atlanta

August 30
TERESA BRAMLETTE
Nexus Contemporary Art Center, Atlanta

GIORGIO BARBERIO CORSETTI (Rome)
is an author and experimental theater director who involves
the public through direct participation, enlarging the space
of conventional theater into the urban environment.

August 18
ERY CAMARA
artist, Mexico City

August 20
BEN APFELBAUM
art consultant, Atlanta

August 24
STEVEN DURLAND
High Performance, North Carolina

August 25
VALERIE ANDERSON
youth participant, Atlanta

August 28
KAREN PALUZZI STEELE
Sculpture Chicago

August 30
JENNIFER MCGREGOR-CUTTING
art advisor, Hartford

PAOLO LANDI (Treviso) is director of communications for Benetton s.p.a., known for its bold, socially directed advertising. He started *Fabrica*, a school for the development of new technical and conceptual languages in media, art, and culture.

August 18
NED RIFKIN
High Museum of Art, Atlanta

August 19
JENNIFER DOWLEY
National Endowment for the Arts, Washington, D.C.

August 24
KOJO GRIFFIN
artist, Atlanta

August 25
BILL CLEVELAND
Walker Art Center, Minneapolis

August 28
MEL CHIN
University of Georgia, Athens

August 30
JACK BECKER
Forecast Public Artworks and *Public Art Review*, St. Paul

EMILIO FANTIN
(Bologna) is an artist who under the name "Emilio Fantin Diffusion" directs the movement of the art audience, physically and mentally, recasting moments and places in life.

August 18
TOMAS YBARRA-FRAUSTO
The Rockefeller Foundation, New York

August 19
MARY JANE JACOB
curator, Chicago

August 20
SUSAN VOGEL
Yale University Art Gallery, New Haven

August 24
ELIZABETH MACGREGOR
IKON Gallery, Birmingham, England

August 25
STEVEN DURLAND
High Performance, North Carolina

August 28
MERRILL ELAM
Scogin Elam and Bray, Architects, Atlanta

August 30
CHRIS SCOATES
Atlanta College of Art Gallery

ENRICO GHEZZI (Rome) is a movie critic, an art director for RAI 3, and creator of the television program "Blob," a collage of the previous day's news that comments on the media's presentation of contemporary culture.

August 18
GENEVIEVE ARNOLD
artist and patron, Atlanta

August 19
SUSAN VOGEL
Yale University Art Gallery, New Haven

August 24
DARIJA DJAVANOVIC
Save the Children, Atlanta

August 25)
JERRY TIPTON
Boys & Girls Clubs of Metro Atlanta

August 28
JOYCE FERNANDEZ
Sculpture Chicago

August 30
LISA GRAZIOSE CORRIN
Contemporary Museum, Baltimore

GIULIO MACCHI (Rome) is director of the cultural magazine *Sfera*, whose thematic issues bring together the ideas of specialists in different disciplines.

August 18
JACQUELYNN BAAS
Berkeley Art Museum, University of California

August 19
JACQUELYNN BASS

August 20
ELENA MOLA
Fulton County School District, Atlanta

August 24
SUSAN BISHOP
Metro Correctional Institution, Atlanta

August 25
SHANTRAS LAKES
High Museum of Art, Atlanta

August 28
PHILIP AUSLANDER
Georgia Institute of Technology, Atlanta

August 30
NICHOLAS DRAKE
critic, Charleston

ANGELA VETTESE (Milan) is an art critic who writes for the daily *Il Sole 24 Ore* and art journals, focusing on work that departs from the market system and expands the place of art today.

August 18
JENNIFER DOWLEY
National Endowment for the Arts, Washington, D.C.

August 19
ANDY AMBROSE
Atlanta History Center

August 24
ANNA HARDING
Goldsmiths College, University of London

August 25
STEFANIA MANTOVANI
artist, Venice

August 28
CATHY BYRD
critic, Atlanta

August 30
ANNE PASTERNAK
Creative Time, New York

MASSIMO CACCIARI (Venice) is a philosopher and the mayor of Venice whose pragmatic and intellectual approach to governing has transformed the office of mayor into a more humanized and publicly concerned post benefiting citizens.

August 18
VISHAKHA DESAI
Asia Society, New York

August 19
DANIEL MARTINEZ
artist, Los Angeles

August 20
ERY CAMARA
artist, Mexico City

August 24
GLENN HARPER
Sculpture Magazine, Washington, D.C.

August 25
DARRYL MAPP
youth participant, Atlanta

August 30
CARRIE PRYZBILLA
High Museum of Art, Atlanta

FRANCESCO PURINI (Rome) is professor of architectural drawing at the Istituto Universitario di Architettura di Venezia. He refers to himself as a "visionary rationalist," believing that architectural concepts must continually be revised to respond to historical contexts.

August 18
ELLEN MEYER
Atlanta College of Art

August 19
LOUISE SHAW
Nexus Contemporary Art Center, Atlanta

August 20
JOANNE CUBBS
High Museum of Art, Atlanta

August 24
FEDERICA THIENE
artist, Venice

August 25
MAURICIO DIAS
artist, Basel

August 28
ANNE BALSAMO
Georgia Institute of Technology, Atlanta

August 30
PATRICIA PHILLIPS
State University of New York, New Paltz

MICHELE SERRA (Bologna) is a writer who addresses the Italian social and political scene for *Cuore settimanale di resistenza umana*, a satire magazine he helped found.

August 18
MICHAEL BRENSON
critic, New York

August 19
MAURICE O'CONNELL
artist, Dublin

August 20
JANICE MORRILL
Atlanta History Center

August 24
ANNE MORGAN
critic, Gainesville

August 25
MARY ELLEN STROM
artist, New York

August 30
JESSICA CUSSICK
Cultural Arts Council of Houston

CONVERSATIONS
ON CULTURE

SUNDAY, AUGUST 18, 6:00 P.M.

Session Leader:

MICHAEL BRENSON

Topic:

CONVERSATION

Location:

HEARTFIELD MANOR, 182 ELIZABETH STREET

The conversation took place in a room of a turn-of-the-century, craftsman-style home in Atlanta's historic Inman Park. This intimate setting contains antique furniture, books, and family photographs.

Method of Preparation:

COMPOSTA

On the first evening the food and table setting underlined the concept of "conversations": each dish was constructed of many little parts, built one upon the other. Thus, the method rather than the type of food was important. If conversations are the result of interactions and integration, then the menu for this evening — like ideas into words, words into phrases, phrases into sentences — was created of food in many parts. The table was set with a handmade cotton tablecloth and white ceramic dishes. The meal was placed in the center of the table and shared among the guests according to the time and rhythm of the conversation. The dessert was thought of like a photograph of the group: on the occasion of a dinner among friends, instead of a Polaroid, "Le Faccie di Crema" (plates of pudding with fruit) carried the portraits of the guests.

Menu:

PROSECCO PRIMO FRANCO

SHISH KEBAB
WITH FRUIT AND CHEESE
FISH AND VEGETABLES
MEAT AND VEGETABLES

INSALATA DOLCE

INSALATA DI MARE

MACEDONIA

FRAGOLINO BIANCO

"LE FACCIE DI CREMA"

ESPRESSO ILLY

GRAPPA

CONVERSATION

By definition, conversation is a hopeful word. It is an assurance that trust is possible, that listening can be as creative as speaking, that people can be open about their vulnerability and doubt and not be ridiculed or dismissed. The existence of the word suggests that the us-them, insider-outsider mentality, which has been ingrained in art museums and the news media and unwittingly reinforced by theoretical buzzwords like "audience" and "public," is not inevitable, and that bridges between people are as natural as walls. The currency of expressions like bringing so-and-so "into the conversation," or initiating a "national conversation" on issues like culture or race, is an indication of the widespread longing for an alternative to the politics of accusation and demonization that have made election campaigns, as well as exchanges about almost every major national issue, demoralizing. For John Dewey, belief in the "possibility of conducting disputes, controversies, and conflicts as co-operative undertakings in which both parties learn by giving the other a chance to express itself, instead of having one party conquer by forceful suppression of the other" was essential to the democratic faith.[1] "To take as far as possible every controversy which arises — and they are bound to arise — out of the atmosphere and medium of force, of violence as a means of settlement, into that of discussion and of intelligence," Dewey wrote in "Creative Democracy," "is to treat those who disagree — even profoundly — with us as those from whom we may learn, and in so far, as friends." For Primo Levi, who struggled for forty years to grasp the lessons and meanings of Auschwitz, where he had witnessed perhaps the ultimate consequences of demonization, discussion was essential to progress and justice. In *Facing the Extreme*, subtitled *Moral Life in the Concentration Camps*, Tsvetan Todorov makes a passionate argument against the Manichaenism that gives license to the most sinister discrimination and brutality, and for the value, even when one has little or no stomach for it, of communication. Discussing a courageous and necessary book that grew out of interviews between British journalist Gitta Sereny and Franz Stengel, a Nazi she abhorred, Todorov writes: "To talk *with* someone rather than *about* him implies that I recognize a commonality with that person even if my words are incompatible in meaning with his."[2]

Conversation is fundamental. It is part of the machinery of culture, of society, of the self. It stretches the imagination and makes it possible to envisage new narratives at the end of a century in which some of the most controlling master narratives have collapsed. It shapes almost everyone's notion — or dream — of friendship and family. It shapes the creative visions of musicians, poets, community leaders, and politicians. It is not just actual conversations that are decisive. Artists of all kinds establish imaginary conversations with other artists within their work. I cannot imagine the process of thinking apart from conversation. The way I work out an essay or lecture always involves

1
John Dewey, "Creative Democracy — The Task Before Us," in *The Collected Works of John Dewey, 1882–1953: The Later Works*, vol. 14 (Carbondale: Southern Illinios University Press, 1991), 224.

2
The book is Sereny's *Into That Darkness*. Stangl was the former commandant of both Sobibor and Treblinka. See Tsvetan Todorov, *Facing the Extreme: Moral Life in the Concentration Camps* (New York: Metropolitan Books, 1996), 279.

internalized as well as real conversations with other writers or friends. While sitting with a notepad or at the keyboard, I will arrive at an idea and then find myself thinking about critics or artists with whom that idea is identified and then engage them in questions and answers as the idea develops or dissolves. Internalized conversations with people I admire, and sometimes also with people who have made their disrespect for me clear, are a part of my daily life — on subways, on planes, while walking the streets. "My consciousness is an internalization of the discourse of others," Todorov wrote. "The 'I' is formed by the 'they.'"[3] In the United States, however, where Madison Avenue and the news media feed off the image of a heroically self-sufficient, self-generating individualism, the role of conversation in the formation of the individual is easily overlooked. It is hard to market the awareness that within the fabric of the individual is always a community. It is even harder for any system that expects its leaders to know all the answers to acknowledge that this community never consists solely of people who reflect aspects of ourselves to which we admit. We are formed by contact with people who are different from as well as similar to us. People who challenge or deny us are parts of our inner communities as well as friends. Any project that is structured around conversation as searchingly and as ritualistically as "Conversations at The Castle" marks the presence of others and of the other in the "I." It celebrates the communal nature of our ever-evolving consciousness.

But we need to be careful. The word conversation has a feel-good ring that promises easy answers. The difficulties and risks involved in engaging in conversation can be considerable. And despite the apparent simplicity and directness of the word, its meanings are far from transparent. Conversation can have many forms and functions. It can be extremely stylized. It can be what happens when strangers meet in a bar. It can be a way in which boys or girls, men or women, try to convince someone they are courting that they are really warm, caring souls. "You can trust me, you can talk to me," the predatory adolescent in Larry Clark's film *Kids* says to virgins whose reluctance to sleep with him he is trying to break down. Conversation can be a way of cloaking a punitive act in the rhetoric of concern. "Come into my office, we need to talk" is the ruse principals use with students in trouble and bosses use with employees they are about to fire. Conversation can be the means by which journalists chat someone up in order to get that person to say something incriminating. When I worked for *The New York Times*, I was fascinated by the ability of one top editor to draw someone into conversation and to know exactly when the guest had reached a point of defenseless ease, with no choice but to answer the question that finally revealed the intent of the meeting. Conversation can also be what takes place during a business lunch, the success of which often depends upon obedience to a code defined by the strictest rules about who can say what to whom and when, and what can and cannot be revealed.

While the prevalence of the word in the mid-1990s almost suggests a national longing for a kind of communication that can point beyond the ideological viciousness that has turned so many discussions during the culture wars into combat, conversations are definitely not free of ideology. The need in the United States to talk openly about emotions and feelings comes more from

3
Todorov,
*Facing the Extreme,*104.

Brenson

women than from men. It comes more from those who feel their realities have been silenced or repressed. It comes more from groups trying to be heard than from those in power. You don't hear conservatives like Jesse Helms, Dick Armey, or Hilton Kramer, who are convinced they possess the truth and have no intention of allowing it to be challenged, expressing a hunger for conversation. People in power on the Left as well as the Right may be reluctant to exchange feelings and thoughts if they feel they and only they have something to lose in the conversation. While on assignment for *The Times*, I found from time to time that people who worked for institutions I was visiting experienced my conversational manner, which seemed to me perfectly natural, as a violation, as putting them on the spot; to converse was to be exposed, and if they were going to express themselves openly, even on subjects that seemed to me inconsequential, they had to be certain I would respect their vulnerable positions. Conversation can certainly be a means of exploitation or repression. We all know people who have skillfully adopted controlling conversational styles as ways of *preventing* genuine communication from taking place. We all know institutional authorities who attempt to draw those who oppose their policies into conversation not in order to respond to their grievances but as a way of neutralizing them. I'm sure that the benevolent missionary approach that made it possible for Christians to violate people different from them and conceal their violence from themselves was conversational.

In short, although the word is wrapped in an aura of reciprocity and acceptance, conversation, as often as not, is a form of manipulation. Many conversations are astonishingly complex mixtures of candor and performance. Most have an agenda determined by the person or the side who initiated it and set the terms. Most, even those as good-natured and free-wheeling as exchanges in locker rooms, car pools, and diners, are extremely conventionalized in ways that make certain kinds of communication possible, but others not. Only in conversations with the most trusted loved ones and friends — and perhaps not even then — can everything that someone may want to say actually be said. Conversations can be disheartening as well as inspiring. Every conversation, even the most liberating, depends upon conventions that people from some backgrounds have an easier time mastering than others. The kind of conversation I will advocate here may be as strange to people of other religions and races as their conventions of conversation may be to me. While the conventions vary from family to family, neighborhood to neighborhood, and culture to culture, however, I strongly believe conversation is so indispensable throughout the world that discussing the idea with citizens of countries as different as, let's say, Senegal, Switzerland, Slovenia, and Brazil would make communication, if not conversation, across cultures possible.

There is little use in condemning stylized or manipulative conversations, or in arguing that some kinds are authentic and others are not. Together they reveal not only the multitude of conversations through which each individual's and each society's awareness is shaped, but also the multitude of conversations that may exist within each conversation. They are clues to the density and difficulty but also to the richness and fluidity of our private and interconnective worlds. There is no unmediated spontaneity. The masters of dialogue in fiction have understood that all conversa-

123

tions, creative or destructive, empathetic or deceitful, are governed by codes or rules. So have film-makers such as Satyajit Ray and Eric Rohmer, who have made clear that conversation is an art that has to be understood by anyone wanting to communicate effectively across class and gender, and by so doing to define with maximum clarity his or her place in society. And even the most codified conversations can have beneficial results: conversational rituals like business lunches can demand such attentiveness and style that genuine bonds can be created from them. Functioning well in any industrialized nation, or perhaps anywhere else for that matter, requires respecting that different contexts demand different conversations and being able to maintain the kind of conversation each situation demands.

Once the fundamental importance of conversation has been recognized and the complexity of the word acknowledged, I can define the kind I believe is most valuable, which is the kind I think the majority of the people who came to Atlanta to participate in "Conversations at The Castle" were after. This conversation is informal and flexible. It is driven not by the desire to reinforce entrenched positions but by a need for common probing. It is driven by a belief in the value of attentiveness. Listening not only mobilizes conversation but also makes it a creative force. It gives the potential at each moment for surprise and transformation. It enables participants to feel they are taken seriously even when others disagree with them. As long as the responses resonate with what has just been spoken and heard, there are few limits on what can be expressed, and criticism or questioning will not descend into personal attack. This conversation may have an agenda, but it is one that can be shaped by everyone present. Power is shared. This does not mean that in the course of the exchanges people who have more knowledge and who see some issues more clearly will not have authority over others. However, their influence is earned. What it also means is that the power relationships within the conversation are unstable, that they can shift at any moment, and that imposition of power is not the objective of any participant.

While this kind of exchange of feelings and thoughts is widely understood as being, by its nature, an alternative to violence, it must not exclude the possibility of aggression and conflict. It cannot be conversation at its fullest unless every participant knows he or she has the right to speak openly and, if need be, with anger. Everyone also has the right to speak up without worrying if the others present will find his or her responses stupid. The most sustaining conversations depend as much upon a suspension of judgment as they do upon direct engagement and nuanced concern. They also depend upon a capacity for self-criticism, both within the individual and the group. Participants must be able to hear the challenges to them. While participants in a conversation are not obliged to question its assumptions and justifications, the conversation must be open to analysis at any moment. Just as important, in the most meaningful conversation the burden for success, which in large measure depends upon safeguarding the freedom and confidence of each participant, is accepted by everyone present. This kind of conversation requires responsibility as well as risk and work.

When this kind of give-and-take exists, it has intrinsic value. It becomes an end as well as a means. Process becomes product. The conversation becomes a tissue of connectedness that may turn out to be more substantial and enduring than any intellectual resolution it may have achieved. I don't remember who was hired as a result of some of the search committees on which I have served, but I remember vividly those conversational hours in which each person gave himself or herself freely and fully for months. I have no idea what a friend and I spoke about during a long descent down Mount Washington forty years ago, but as a result of the openness and warmth of that dialogue I will always remember the descent and her. In the twenty-five years of my friendship with Jonathan, a Reagan Republican, we never agreed on anything political but talked constantly and freely about almost everything. I never changed his political views and he never changed mine, but our effect on each other was profound, and the intensity and breadth of our conversations sustains me years after his death. The one time Jonathan met Irving, a Marxist and the other closest friend of my adult life, they spoke passionately all evening. What they had in common was curiosity, introspectiveness, suppleness of mind, and a love of intensely engaged conversation. These kinds of exchanges of energy and commitment, of speaking and listening, of reaction and perception, concentrate space and time. They have for me a poetic intensity that is not different in nature from the intensity of my encounters with painting and sculpture.

Conversation, at its fullest, illuminates the aesthetic. It can generate an aesthetic experience that may not be as self-contained and therefore as physical as one's encounters with painting and sculpture, but it can take on a comparable resonance and eventually may inhabit the same region of the imagination. Like the give-and-take between a viewer and a painting or sculpture, conversation of the profoundest kind depends upon and therefore draws out virtues like attentiveness, goodness, generosity, and commitment. It also makes each person who partakes of it feel part of something larger than his or her individual self. Like my experience of a Brancusi sculpture, for example, or of a painting by Malevich or Mondrian, conversation can create a sense of infinite possibility within the here and now. Through conversation, a connection that is worthy of careful investigation can be made between, on one hand, the aesthetic and, on the other hand, the composition and potential of self and culture.

My first model for art was conversational. With van Gogh and Cézanne, the two artists I have loved since my father first took me to The Museum of Modern Art when I was a child, the conversations have been constant. I see their work, it says something to me, I respond, it responds. Over the years my questions change; so do its answers. My conversations with these and many other artists will never end. The idea of art as dialogue — not as the divine spirit or Word being passed down (as in so much of the religious art I also need) but as a mutual exchange — is modernist. It began to shape art during that post-impressionist moment when Cézanne felt the world was no longer knowable through established classifications. It had to be empirically reexamined, seen each day as if from scratch. In Cézanne's paintings, this examination took the form of a sustained poetic conversation in which the process of perceiving, doubting, and recording came to define not only the structure of the painting but also the way it was experienced. Partly because there were

125

Brenson

so many layers of conversation in the work's formation, there are many layers of conversation in the response to it. Because of Cézanne the conversational process is part of cubism and everything that comes out of it, including abstract art wherein continuing personal discovery is of paramount importance. Part of the modernist faith was that the conversational exchange built into the experience of art would help bring into being a more open and inventive relationship between individuals and their social and spiritual environments.

Obviously, the modernist model developed in a world very different from the one in which we live. "Conversations at The Castle" was conceived with a full awareness of that model's limits. To me, however, a program constructed around actual conversations in Atlanta between artists from outside the United States and individuals and communities not normally engaged by museum art is not a repudiation of modernism but both a radical critique and extension of it. Many artists who shaped modernism believed in a fundamental link between artistic necessity and human transformation. Many modernists believed that the materials and ways of seeing passed down to them were inadequate to deal with the human and artistic challenges they faced, and that in order to have any chance of maintaining its vitality the past had to be rigorously questioned as it was being assimilated and reimagined. Modernists consistently challenged institutional thinking and interests, in part by taking ever more seriously realities — like those of children, or the working classes, or non-Western cultures — that had been considered superficially, if at all, by Western artists before them.

But modernism went only so far. Only rarely were working-class men and women, men and women from non-Western societies, or young people — not to speak of women and those of African descent — welcomed into the debates about whom art was for, how it could heal and transform, and what it could be. One of the consequences of the culture wars is that many arts professionals now recognize that some of the voices and cultures that helped inspire the modernist imagination constitute audiences with views of art that have little or nothing to do with modernism or with museums, and these are audiences upon which they increasingly depend. Even more challenging to the purpose, if not to the soul of these institutions, many members of these audiences believe that far from wanting to initiate conversations with them, modernism and museums are determined to leave them out. "Conversations at The Castle" was informed by a conviction that art could be available to everyone, and that if it did become a way of building and reinforcing communication among segments of society that have remained largely cut off from one another, both art and democracy would be strengthened. When artistic and curatorial imaginations are applied to the development of interaction among actual people, challenging all participants both to confront real life situations and to transform them through an enhanced communal understanding, conversation is revealed as an activity that is indispensable to an inclusive vision. It is also revealed as an activity that exposes, and therefore makes it easier to develop, connections among the political, the spiritual, and the aesthetic. If there is one need most worth exploring now, it may be conversation.

126

Brenson

MONDAY, AUGUST 19, 6:00 P.M.

Session Leader:

JACQUELYNN BAAS

Topic:

AUDIENCE AND INSTITUTIONS

Location:

WOODRUFF ARTS CENTER
PEACHTREE AND FIFTEENTH STREETS NE

The evening's conversation took place on the balcony level above the grand atrium in the city's cultural complex that is home to the High Museum of Art, Atlanta College of Art and Design, Alliance Theater, and Symphony Hall. In its modern design and use of marble, steel, glass, and carpets, this space evokes the official nature of such established institutions.

Method of Preparation:

CONSERVAZIONE

On the second evening the menu was developed to underline how much the art world, as represented by established institutions, is specialized and far from the reality of the public. And so, the food was very specialized, traditional, typical, and of difficult flavor, far from common tastes. The menu was traditional Venetian cuisine characteristic of the artists' and chef's home. A Venetian dessert, *tiramisu* (sometimes translated as "cheer me up"), was served with best wishes to the institutions. The menu, food preparation, table setting, and serving of each course was carried out by the artists and assistants without the participation of the guests. The table was covered with a white cotton *filo di Francia* lace tablecloth made at one of the artist's family home and set with formal, white ceramic plates.

Menu:

PROSECCO PRIMO FRANCO

FRITTATINA DI CIPOLLA

COZZE E VONGOLE SALTATE

PASTA E FAGOLI

BACCALA ALLA VICENTINA CON POLENTA

VERZA SOFEGADA

FRAGOLINO BIANCO

TIRAMISU

ESPRESSO ILLY

GRAPPA

JACQUELYNN BAAS

CITADELS OF INCLUSIVE AWARENESS

Ours is the first age in which many thousands of the best-trained individual minds have made it a full-time business to get inside the collective public mind. To get inside in order to manipulate, exploit, control is the object now. And to generate heat not light is the intention.... But the time for anger and protest is in the early stages of a new process. The present stage is extremely advanced. Moreover, it is full, not only of destructiveness but also of promises of rich new developments to which moral indignation is a very poor guide.... Ever since Burckhardt saw that the meaning of Machiavelli's method was to turn the state into a work of art by the rational manipulation of power, it has been an open possibility to apply the method of art analysis to the critical evaluation of society.... Art criticism is free to point to the various means employed to get the effect, as well as to decide whether the effect was worth attempting. As such ... it can be a citadel of inclusive awareness amid the dim dreams of collective consciousness.

—Marshall McLuhan, *The Mechanical Bride: Folklore of Industrial Man*, 1951

The grainy black-and-white, mildly erotic cover of the 1967 paperback edition of Marshall McLuhan's *The Mechanical Bride* happened to be waiting for me on my bedside table when I settled in at the Heartfield Manor on August 16, 1996. That night, before going to sleep, I skimmed the Canadian communications theorist's preface, written at the midpoint of the twentieth century. I was in Atlanta to lead a discussion group on the topic of art institutions and their audiences as part of a series of discussions entitled "Conversations on Culture." McLuhan's book seemed oddly at

JACQUELYNN BAAS received a BA in art history from Michigan State University and an MA and PhD from the University of Michigan. Her academic specialties include the history of prints, nineteenth-century French art, and twentieth-century art and architecture. She has published on a range of subjects, from the nineteenth-century woodcut revival to the postwar British Independent Group to, most recently, the work of Peter Shelton for the Henry Moore Trust (1997). Among her many exhibitions, she is currently co-curating a retrospective exhibition of Joan Brown's work, scheduled to open in fall 1998 concurrently at the University of California, Berkeley Art Museum and the Oakland Museum of California. Baas began her museum career at the University of Michigan Museum of Art, where she served as registrar and assistant director. She went to Dartmouth College as chief curator in 1982 and helped plan and build the Hood Museum of Art, assuming the position of director in 1985. She went on to Berkeley to direct the University Art Museum and Pacific Film Archive in 1989 and was responsible for its re-naming in September 1996 from the "University Art Museum" to the "Berkeley Art Museum," in accordance with a generous and determined anonymous donor's wish to see the museum's community recognized in its name. Baas's interest in museum amenities was stimulated by an offer from renowned Berkeley-based chef (and film fan) Alice Waters to help develop a cafe at the museum, a project currently in planning.

home amid the vintage southern pop-culture decor of the Heartfield Manor. I was glad to see it, as I was casting about for some perspective on three interrelated questions facing art institutions in the 1990s. First, who should our audience be — everybody or only everybody who happens to be interested in art? Second, with our current state of diminished public funding, how can art institutions attract and keep new audiences? And finally, the big question: what is the purpose of art museums now? I knew I could count on McLuhan (always ahead of his time) to provide insight into this interesting cultural moment, three-and-a-half years before the end of the century and the end of a millennium as well.

In the course of thirty years spent studying and working in university art museums, I have become quite fond of these odd and oddly overlooked hybrids of the public realm, with their tradition of public responsibility and academic freedom. It was not particularly noted, for example, that the exhibition "Robert Mapplethorpe: The Perfect Moment," one of the most controversial exhibition events ever, was created by a university art museum, the Institute of Contemporary Art at the University of Pennsylvania. In the winter of 1990 it was shown at the University Art Museum, Berkeley, where I am director. Both the chancellor at the time, Michael Heyman, and then-president David Gardner (who is a Mormon) supported the show. More people saw it there than anywhere else on its tour, and our city council voted unanimously to give the museum a commendation for "courage."

Art is a visual record of the efforts of human beings throughout history to perceive, understand, and interpret the nature of existence. These things of beauty and mystery and even horror enable us to conceive the world and ourselves in new ways. The best museums provide a stimulating place where people can let their customary defenses down and learn to empathize with those who may be quite different from themselves. We live in a society composed of many cultures and from which new cultural expressions are emerging at an astonishing rate. Our society is engaged in the process of trying to reform our social structures to accommodate profound social and cultural change. In this process, it is essential for us to understand one another. But it is difficult to understand a culture without understanding its languages, and one of the most accessible is the artistic language — its vocabulary, syntax, and symbolism. To use an academic metaphor, museums have the potential to be the language labs of cultural understanding.

McLuhan considered his gimlet-eyed analysis of postwar advertising to be a kind of art criticism. But perhaps his most effective heirs have been not art critics but artists like Hans Haacke and (among my fellow conversationists on the topic of audiences and institutions the night of August 19) younger artists such as Doug Ashford, Daniel Martinez, and Maurice O'Connell, whose works foreground and implicitly or explicitly critique forms of social and cultural manipulation. These artists spoke of the irony of how community-based art practice and social critique have become bureaucratized, institutionalized by museums and other cultural organizations. Despite the paradox of this situation, traditional public spaces, such as town squares, parks, and streets are now so programmed, so controlled, that art museums may be one of the few remaining sites for free artistic expression and for, as Ashford put it, "random, nonrational interaction with art." The private

130

realm of the art institution has become the primary locus for artistic statements about public as well as private issues. With their recent emphasis on multicultural and cross-cultural exhibitions and education programs, art museums may well be, in McLuhan's words, the last "citadels of inclusive awareness amid the dim dreams of collective consciousness."

The session began with a discussion of the 1996 Atlanta Olympics, or more precisely with the art of spectacle, of which the 1996 Olympics seemed to be the quintessential example. Mediated events like the Olympics and surrogate experiences now provided by "real" places like Las Vegas, as well as fantasy places like Disneyland, are designed for maximum financial exploitation of their increasingly large audiences. In an effort to compete for audience attention within the spectacle atmosphere of the Olympics, Ned Rifkin, director of Atlanta's High Museum of Art (also present at our conversation) hired National Gallery of Art director emeritus J. Carter Brown to organize "Rings: Five Passions in World Art": an "extraordinary assemblage of artworks spanning seven millennia and the principal regions of the world."[1]

Brown's name recognition, as well as that of many of the artists in his show, attracted large crowds undaunted by the scorn of art world critics. Not knowing quite what to expect but wanting to see and judge the show for myself, I found the experience of "Rings" to be almost pure pleasure. I encountered one ravishing work of art after another, each challenging me to analyze my responses to the art and to Brown's construction of "five interlocking passions that have fascinated artists the world over": love, anguish, awe, triumph, and joy. "Triumph" seemed a suspect category constructed for its Olympian context, while the works in "joy" felt somewhat wan in comparison with those in the first three sections. But it took me about five minutes in the exhibition to figure out that for the next couple of hours I was going to be a very happy person.

In my experience, no other art exhibition, except perhaps Nayland Blake and Larry Rinder's weirdly similar exhibition of gay culture "In A Different Light," presented at The University Art Museum, Berkeley, in the winter of 1995, seemed to demand so little of me while offering so much.[2] Although the socio-political ambitions of "In A Different Light" and the aesthetic pretensions of "Rings" could hardly have been more different, both exhibitions were organized in terms of emotional or psychic conditions, seducing viewers into engagement with the art while testing their responses against those of the organizers. The nature of this engagement was experiential rather than intellectual, producing a feisty mental state very different from the earnest viewer attitudes engendered by more didactically organized art exhibitions. No matter what the context, works of art can catch us unawares, propelling us into unexpected states of delight or intuitive understanding. It's largely in the hope of such an experience that many people go to art museums. "Rings" and "In A Different Light" both behaved in this fashion as exhibitions: I didn't "go through" them; I had a relationship with them. Despite their idiosyncrasies and occasional irritations, I left each a different person than when I went in.

As for "Rings," one thing was certain: although the show partook of the culture of spectacle personified by the concurrent Olympics, it was an event that resisted mediation; "Rings" had to be

1
On view at the High Museum of Art from July 4 to September 29, 1996. The quotation is from the dust jacket of the exhibition catalogue. J. Carter Brown and Michael E. Shapiro, eds., *Rings: Five Passions in World Art* (New York: Harry N. Abrams and the High Museum of Art, 1996).

2
The dust jacket of the book states, "Instead of inquiring 'what does lesbian or gay art look like?' the curators ask: 'How are queer artists looking at the world?'" Nayland Blake, Lawrence Rinder, and Amy Scholder, eds., *In A Different Light: Visual Culture, Sexual Identity, Queer Practice* (San Francisco: City Lights Books, 1995). The exhibition was divided into nine sections: void, self, drag, other, couple, family, orgy, world, and utopia.

experienced to be experienced. If there is a difference between a media event and an art museum exhibition — any exhibition — it ought to come down to this sequential, contextual, sensual process. One has to be in an exhibition, among works of art that act on us one by one through all the nuances of their actual presence. The Internet won't do; a slide lecture won't do; the catalogue won't do; neither will a CD-ROM or video. Helpful as these mediating devices can be, they are essentially deductive in nature. Art, on the other hand, is inherently empirical.

Despite their profound differences as art events, "In a Different Light," "Rings," and "Conversations at The Castle" all felt to me like "gifts," to cite the title of Lewis Hyde's 1979 book, *The Gift: Imagination and the Erotic Life of Property*. I had been drawn to this book (itself a gift from my former deputy director, Bonnie Pitman) in thinking about the context for "Conversations on Culture." Venetian artists Federica Thiene and Stefania Mantovani of the collective artway of thinking were organizing a series of carefully orchestrated dinners to provide an aesthetic channel for communication in support of the conversations. Hyde's epigraph from the Taittiriya Upanishad paralleled my fantasy of the atmosphere *Chow for "Conversations on Culture"* might produce. It locates consumption at the center of our spiritual existence, a concept quite at odds with current negative associations of this word with capitalist exploitation through commodification.

> O wonderful! O wonderful! O wonderful!
> I am food! I am food! I am food!
> I eat food! I eat food! I eat food!
> My name never dies, never dies, never dies!
> I was born first in the first of the words,
> earlier than the gods, in the belly of what has no death!
> Whoever gives me away has helped me the most!
> I, who am food, eat the eater of food!
> I have overcome this world!
> He who knows this shines like the sun.
> Such are the laws of the mystery![3]

3
Lewis Hyde, *The Gift: Imagination and the Erotic Life of Property* (New York: Vintage Books, 1983), xix.

According to Hindu philosophy, the world is an endless cycle of eating and being eaten — we consume food and our bodies "cook" it, transform it into brain and bone and flesh and energy. But we are consumed in turn, transformed into other forms of energy, be they food or fire. Whoever understands this cyclical nature of life — the fundamental reality that "I, who am food, eat the eater of food" — transcends the cycle and is free to be released by the ultimate fire, the fire of the spirit. Should not what we call the "perception" of art be more properly termed "consumption"? What would be the implications of such a shift in nomenclature? Among other things, art might be more clearly understood as food for the soul rather than as a commodity.

Hyde surely chose his quotation for the line "Whoever gives me away has helped me the most." It accords with his theory that a work of art is experienced as a gift, not a commodity: "A commodity has value and a gift does not. A gift has worth." That worth is multiplied, not used up,

132

by sharing; the artist renews the source of his or her creativity by sharing it with others. And for those who experience art, that experience feels like a gift, even if it is paid for through purchase or the payment of an exhibition admission fee. The work of art can exist in the realm of the commodity as well as the realm of gift exchange, but the balance is a fragile one. If the felt presence of manipulation or exploitation is stronger than the aesthetic presence, the aesthetic experience never happens. To judge from the critical response to "Rings" versus the response of its lay audience, the location of this threshold varies considerably.

Now, nothing could have been more different from the pleasantly bombastic "Rings" than the pleasantly subversive *Chow*, which used the preparation, serving, and appreciation of food as an art medium. (My most startling aesthetic insight during the two *convivi*-dinners in which I took part was the moment when we were served surprise pudding desserts that were caricatures of ourselves, merrily breaking up our seemingly endless discussion of the effects of identity on communication.) "Rings" had a huge audience, "Conversations at The Castle" a small one. Yet, both felt like gifts — "Rings" because of the quality and variety of the artworks that had been gathered from around the world for my enjoyment and that of thousands of my fellow humans, "Conversations" because of the generosity and care in execution that informed the project at all levels. Both of them altered my perception of the world and of myself. And both were made possible by established art institutions: the High Museum of Art and the Arts Festival of Atlanta. As different from each other as they are, both of these institutions seem important to the cultural and spiritual health of Atlanta.

The experience of *Chow for "Conversations on Culture"* stimulated my thinking on whether museums could become more holistic institutions and, if so, how. In her 1992 book *Systems of Survival*, Jane Jacobs provides a model for the role of art in society that is quite different from Hyde's. By analyzing moral judgments in published news accounts of behavior, Jacobs (a Canadian like McLuhan) perceived two distinct, in fact contradictory, ethical systems underlying contemporary society. The "guardian syndrome" arose, according to Jacobs, from behaviors relating to foraging for food and guarding territory. The "commercial syndrome" has its more recent origins in trade and the production of goods. Each has its set of values, values that contradict each other even as they coexist in contemporary society. Among the moral values of the guardian syndrome are: be exclusive, adhere to tradition, make rich use of leisure, shun trading, dispense largesse. The commercial syndrome has an opposing set of values: be open to novelty, use initiative and enterprise, be thrifty, be industrious, trade and compete.

Art, Jacobs argues, was originally a product of the guardian syndrome, related to the precept to "make rich use of leisure." According to Jacobs, art is fundamentally ecological. If a group hunts and forages or makes war continuously, it will quickly deplete itself. Thus, the "value" of diversions such as artistic expression that feed the spirit while sparing the environment. Though Jacobs does not discuss museums specifically, they would seem by definition to be a product of the guardian syndrome as well. The shift of museums from the guardian to the commercial realm, in terms of the composition of their boards and staffs and their resulting policies and behavior, might be proposed as a source of our recent instinctive discomfort. There is an immense shift taking place — from one value system toward another. For example, I suspect I am not alone in feeling there is something oxymoronic about the concept of museum marketing, although I am hard-pressed to explain this feeling in logical terms. What could be wrong with bringing art institutions to the attention of the broadest possible audience by using the most effective methods? Could the instinctive conflict I feel be a conflict between two ethical systems, between commercial marketing techniques and traditional guardian strictures to "shun trading" or "be exclusive" — strictures that were part of my early museum training?

The practice of naming museums and the spaces and positions within them for people whose largesse supports these institutions is hardly new; both museums and universities have been using this time-honored device for raising building and endowment funds for several centuries. Then why did this topic incite such passion among those participating in our conversation on audience and institutions? What is the significance, for example, of the Los Angeles Museum of Contemporary Art's rechristening its beloved T. C. (the former MOCA at the Temporary Contemporary) The Geffen Contemporary at MOCA in return for a gift of five million dollars? Has David Geffen "bought" the T. C. in some fashion, or is MOCA simply following an effective and long-accepted fundraising practice by acknowledging the generosity of a donor? The group worried this topic from every possible angle. Is the public disenfranchised, in fact or in perception, when a donor "buys" the name of a public cultural institution? The answers to this question are surely as various as art institutions themselves. But what I perceived as a new level of alarm may be another manifestation of our discomfort with the shift of museums from the guardian to the commercial realm. What was previously understood as a relatively benign practice when museums were felt primarily to be guardians of culture becomes profoundly threatening in an institution that is actively engaged in creating and marketing a product, especially when that product is culture.

It is important for art institutions to understand and integrate the complex aspects of this shift. When museums blur the significant difference between marketing their collections and exhibitions to audiences that would otherwise not know of them and marketing product spin-offs of these same collections and exhibitions through venues such as the shopping channel and web sites that are little more than electronic shopfronts for the museum store, integration begins to look like exploitation. No one is in a better position to exploit art than art museums. The temptation is strong, for the new reality is that museums and other art institutions are trying to do more with less funding. It is the classic museum conundrum — preservation versus access — with a new twist. Today, the challenge is not just how to preserve and present art objects but how to work with our communities to develop ways in which collections can attract traditionally underserved audiences. Our responsibilities now extend not just to our actual audience but to our "potential audience," to use Ned Rifkin's phrase. With the help of charitable foundation funding initiatives aimed at developing new audiences, museums have joined "many thousands of the best trained individual minds" making it their business, in McLuhan's words, "to get inside the collective public mind."

Unfortunately, funding for exhibitions has diminished even as funding for audience analysis, marketing, and outreach programs has increased. Moreover, these shifts in patterns of support have opened up new realms of expensive responsibilities such as the creation and maintenance of community advisory committees, "professional" marketing, and evaluation by consultants. The need for unrestricted income to support exhibitions and general operating costs has encouraged expansive entrepreneurial activities such as "space rental," "destination restaurants," and larger museum stores. Beyond generating needed income, such entrepreneurship can hold potential for furthering the museum's mission. The use of museum spaces for social and religious rituals such as weddings and bar mitzvahs can help integrate an art institution within a community. Food connects, as we saw in *Chow for "Conversations on Culture."* Done right, it nourishes a sense of community and rewards an aesthetic sensibility through taste, texture, and design. At the very least, good conversation or good thought over a cup of coffee can reinforce or prepare one for an aesthetic experience, and browsing through books or even postcards can promote an engaged intellectual state. In other words, museums can use this moment of change to engage the whole person. The best museums think about their income-generating activities as they think about their exhibitions, as ways to simultaneously enhance public life and nourish the private self. In order to avoid the exploitation of art and to treat audiences with dignity and hospitality, museums need to apply the same high level of creativity and thoughtfulness to their retail activities as to their artistic programs.

Finally, the question we must seriously ask ourselves is whether we are generating light or only heat. The museum conundrum at the end of the millennium would seem to be maintaining the creative tension between keeping (in the English sense in which curators are "keepers") and giving; to present and preserve art with a perceptible spirit of generosity to both the present and the future. Art institutions need to find their own special ways to cultivate Hyde's "spirit of the artist's gift," ways appropriate to changing communities and their particular histories. They need to make real the contradictory concept that "whoever gives me away has helped me the most." A similar tension is contained in McLuhan's "citadel of inclusive awareness." In retrospect, the key word may be not "citadel," with its wary 1950s overtones, or "inclusive," with its prescient perspective, but "awareness," with its Aquarian sense of total consciousness. Perhaps those of us who are part of the continuing process of change in the relation between art institutions and their audiences should recite as our mantra every day Marshall McLuhan's dictum: the moment "is full, not only of destructiveness but also of promises of rich new developments to which moral indignation is a very poor guide."

TUESDAY, AUGUST 20, 6:00 P.M.

Session Leader:

SUSAN VOGEL

Topic:

INTERNATIONAL EXHIBITIONS

Location:

THE CASTLE, 87 FIFTEENTH STREET NE

The site of this conversation was The Castle or, more exactly the exhibition "Conversations at The Castle." Aperitifs were served on the deck, which was also a work of art by Yukinori Yanagi, while the dinner took place in the main meeting room and installation space of Dias and Riedweg on the second floor.

Method of Preparation:

SPECIALE

Cuisine carries the culture of a people and, like the people of a place, is associated with certain geographic territories. It is also the result of exchange and movement among people. For the third evening we limited the form of the food to soup and bread as a method of control to make evident the differences between cultures. Soup and bread share something at their core: they are basic dishes that represent the heart of the cuisine of a culture. Artists participating in "Conversations at The Castle" contributed the menu and assisted in the preparation of the soup and bread from their homelands. The table was set with the plates lent by the participating Italian cultural figures. The dessert, *La Fregolotta*, was a kind of shortcake that is impossible to cut; instead one breaks it with force and then eats it by hand. Here we broke it on Yanagi's "deck of the world" as a wish for unity and the idea of internationality (p. 113).

Menu:

PROSECCO PRIMO FRANCO

ZUPPA DI CIPOLLE AND PANE GENOVESE

CALDINHO DI FEIJAO

GEMUSESUPPE AND BUTTERZOPF

FISH CODDLE AND BROWN SODA BREAD

SOUPOU (NIEKHOU) YEL AK M'BOUROU AND BAGUETTE

BUCKWHEAT SOUP WITH ONION AND HEATHEN COOKIE-BREAD

FRAGOLINO BIANCO

LA FREGOLOTTA

ESPRESSO ILLY

GRAPPA

S U S A N   V O G E L

TRANSLATIONS INTO UNKNOWN LANGUAGES

Translation is at the core of the international exhibition enterprise. Put differently, more or less self-appointed institutions and individuals interpret one culture to another, conferring value and meaning in the process. But the meanings and values themselves are translations. However positive they seem, they cannot be taken for granted as neutral or shared.

From the vantage point of thirty years' experience as a curator and scholar of African art, I would like to reflect on some of the hazards of international exhibitions and to raise questions about curatorial and institutional responsibilities in the translation of cultural ideas, when *traduire c'est trahire* (to translate is to betray) at least to some extent.[1]

For about a century, international art exhibitions have been presumed by their sponsors to serve a benign ambassadorial role, fostering international understanding and respect. But art is inherently ambiguous because the object is visual poetry — allusive, indirect, and mulitlayered no matter how didactic the framing. Because of the experiential nature of exhibitions, the emotional and political nature of cultural identity, and the ambiguous qualities of art, misunderstandings and unintended interpretations are always a risk — and not necessarily benign.

In recent years, questions of cultural ownership and cultural identity increasingly have been debated in public; at the same time they have become more contested and consequential in individual lives. Art exhibitions, almost by definition, make implicit statements about these loaded issues of ownership and identity ("These are treasures, and we have them now"). Coincidentally, at this fraught moment in cultural history, audiences and curators alike are interested in taking chances and may even be eager to venture into difficult terrain. In art exhibitions, the chances of conveying unintended messages are high — and so are the costs of failure. An exhibition is a cryptic form of expression, and exhibitions that confront complex stereotypes or seek to explode popu-

1
Remarks about "international" exhibitions generally apply to any exhibition presenting the art from a culture to an audience that does not identify with that culture. It may generally be less true of solo exhibitions.

SUSAN VOGEL is the Henry J. Heinz II Director of the Yale University Art Gallery. She received her PhD from the Institute of Fine Arts, New York University, and is known for exhibitions and publications on African art and museum issues. She was assistant curator of African art at Nelson Rockefeller's Museum of Primitive Art and became the first curator of African art at the Metropolitan Museum of Art, New York. During her decade there, she made numerous important acquisitions and curated several exhibitions, including the opening installation of the permanent African collection in the Rockefeller Wing. She was founding director of the Museum for African Art, New York, where she curated many influential exhibitions during her ten-year directorship. Her most important exhibitions and publications are: "For Spirits and Kings"; "ART/artifact: African Art in Natural History Collections"; and "Africa Explores: Twentieth-Century African Art." Vogel is completing a major exhibition and book on Baule art of the Ivory Coast based on her extensive field research. "BAULE: African Art/Western Eyes" will open at the Yale Art Gallery in September 1997 and travel to the Art Institute of Chicago and the Museum for African Art, New York.

lar myths can backfire and wind up reinforcing the very misconceptions they address. Museum directors and curators traditionally have sought to insure against offending anyone by blandly avoiding extremes of presentation and skirting around overtly political or emotional subjects. Directors and their trustees talk enthusiastically about risk taking without always accepting the fact that if the risks are genuine, there will be failures.

Art exhibitions are peculiarly ambiguous vehicles for messages that challenge political, historical, or cultural preconceptions, because art objects are by their very nature subjective, equivocal, and capable of multiple readings — especially across cultures. Dan face masks from Liberia, for example, frequently display front teeth between parted lips, teeth that have been filed to points creating a triangular separation in the center. One American graduate student in art history read this Dan sign of beauty as a fearsome sign of aggression, maybe even cannibalism. Even after it had been explained, did it still look to her like the cliché African "scary face"? Likewise, an African visitor to a Brussels cathedral, newly arrived from a village in Mali, was disgusted to see a middle-aged woman gazing rapturously at the sculpture of a nearly naked young man. After this seemingly lascivious spectacle was explained as chaste devotion, what was his interpretation of Christianity and the crucifixion? The visceral reactions of the graduate student and the Malian elder were contradicted by the information they were given. Which was truer? As outsiders, the graduate student and the Malian elder could rightly think they understood a deep truth unseen by a culture immersed in itself. Who will referee this contest of mutually exclusive visions?

Art exhibitions communicate meaning through experience — an unpredictable emotional enterprise under any circumstances. Designers and curators knowingly manipulate the experiential aspects of exhibitions with color, light, texture, pacing, and other tricks all the time. The sanctified halls of a museum create a context with its own significance and conventions rooted in a Western history of classification and display. But fundamental aspects of the exhibition experience are beyond the control of curators because visitors apprehend exhibitions with their physical, intellectual, and emotional idiosyncrasies. As singular persons, they walk through museum halls that feel light or dark, warm or cold, crowded or abandoned, silent or noisy, that are reminiscent of other spaces attached to other emotions. They look at objects, images, and faces that have resonance in their personal histories. They interpret artworks with what they may know about art history, mythology, or religion but even more vividly with individual experiences of gardening, fashion, sex, horsemanship — knowledge gleaned from a whole life. In other words, exhibition visitors arrive with unique, completely unpredictable filters, through which they understand or misunderstand the exhibition.

Curators are aware of this, and we almost automatically address the problem in exhibition planning, reassuring ourselves that we can anticipate the preconceptions and knowledge level of our visitors. Most exhibitions are made for specific audiences in particular places and times and can be tuned to the pitch that suits most of the members of the intended audience. But exhibitions are also available to anyone who appears at the door, making international shows susceptible to misinterpretation.

To return to the examples above, imagine that the Dan mask is included in an American exhibition about the aesthetics of Dan body art and concepts of womanhood arguing that scarification and tooth filing are art forms that create beauty and meaning. Can we assume that the Dan sculptors who made the masks would have framed their intentions that way? Are the values set forth by the exhibition as important to the Dan as they are to the exhibitor? Can we ask American women looking at the mask to accept the belief that women should undergo pain and mutilation to be "beautiful"? Can the curator really insist that scarification and tooth filing must be regarded as art forms and feel confident that the audience will find this persuasive?

Or, suppose our Malian elder sees the crucifix in a museum exhibition dealing with religious imagery of the Northern Renaissance. Can we expect him to accept the curator's interpretation that what looks like sensuous male nudity is an artistic convention that has little to do with eroticism? Are we asking him to suspend his personal values of piety, modesty, and public decency? Above all, can exhibition organizers expect him to agree that the object expresses a set of Christian values when his eyes tell him that these are hypocritical?

Ethical issues are always present in exhibiting, and they take on added complexity when the exhibitions are international. In exhibitions dealing with objects from almost any time or culture except post-Enlightenment Europe, we must confront opposing concepts about the right to know and the right to question. Western museums belong to a culture that prizes openness and the right to see and know all; how do we deal with secret or sacred material, human remains, illicitly excavated or acquired objects, or objects that show the objectionable aspects of a culture? These are not mere philosophical issues but arenas of international contention, forced compromise, and real difference. Our own culture refuses to declare certain areas of knowledge off limits; yet it asks that we respect the convictions of other cultures. The tension between these two conflicting postures is at times unreconcilable; one or the other must sometimes be sacrificed.

In one exhibition I organized, we commissioned a priest to create an altar in the galleries. He asked me to supply him with a human skull as he was having difficulty getting one. The staff and I felt we should not exhibit human remains because it was disrespectful and overly sensational. We learned that real human skulls were legally sold in stores in Manhattan and could be charged on the museum's credit card; what we learned about their sources poisoned these banal facts with an ugly reality. I asked the priest if he would be willing to use a fake skull. I had been thinking of the altar as a work of art and expected the priest to create an object that had the appearance of authenticity. But for him an altar could never be mere appearance. The shrine was sacred, he said, and it would be wrong to put something false in it. He was faithfully making it in the usual way, fulfilling the requirements of the god. Far from disrespectful, he asserted, his request was an expression of respect for the god to whom the shrine was dedicated. I realized that he and I were both reciting the anthem of cultural incomprehension: "Your beliefs are superstition, my beliefs are ethical." We purchased a human skull, and the priest installed a fully functioning altar in the museum. This experience brought home to me the fact that respecting the ethics of others can require true

139

compromise, even the suspension of the curator's own dearly held beliefs — a little-discussed issue in intercultural exhibitions.

The process of creating an exhibition depends on a web of participants, sometimes with conflicting ethics and competing claims on the curator. How does the exhibitor balance responsibilities to artists, audiences, sponsors (financial and moral), and members of the native culture? What about the preservation of art for future generations? When does sensitivity to other points of view amount to sanitizing or self-censorship and when does it represent a betrayal of one's own values?

What about relationships of power and money, the commodification of objects, individuals, and "cultural capital"? The 1991 exhibition "Africa Explores: 20th-Century African Art" included coffins from Ghana in the shapes of huge onions, a Mercedes, and enormous fish. This gave impetus to other museum and gallery shows, which inflated prices both in and outside of Ghana. But this was not enough to transform the carpenter-craftsmen who make them into highly paid artists. On the other hand, this competition from foreign buyers has made the coffins rather expensive for their original purpose: burial. Commodifiction, or as here partial commodification (which may be worse), can follow an international exhibition.

In 1993 I curated an exhibition in Venice and SoHo that suffered from a different problem. It was called "FUSION: West African Artists at the Venice Biennale" and included paintings and sculptures by five university-trained African artists, most of whom lived in Dakar or Abidjan. Its theme was the way African artists have arrived at forms apparently similar but actually different from those produced by twentieth-century artists in Europe and America. The labels — short biographies and quotes from the artists — revealed a social and ideological origin so different from New York or Venice that the objects demanded to be regarded on different terms.

Yet I suspect many visitors saw the paintings and sculptures as what they expected to see, not what I had mounted in the galleries and certainly not what the artists had made. Few people read all the labels in any exhibition, and some people read none at all; some read and disagree. I fear many visitors to "FUSION" left with their prejudices intact, still convinced that contemporary African art is derivative and passé. Had exposure to these works merely reinforced the preconceptions the exhibition attempted to refute? If so, had the execution failed, or was this an impossible project to begin with? Are some assumptions too deep or too ambiguous to be challenged by art exhibitions, especially international ones where the leap of translation is the greatest?

"FUSION: West African Artists at the Venice Biennale" and exhibitions like it, with all their potential for confusion, still have to be attempted — not quixotically, in support of a lost cause, or blithely, ignoring pitfalls — but with the conviction that the chances of success are good and the costs of failure are tolerable. I am confident that these exhibitions can make a dent, however small, create a doubt, however tiny, in a mass belief that will eventually erode. No single exhibition, book, play, film — not even a decade of them — can decenter the belief that all art originating outside the metropolitan centers of Western culture is provincial, imitative, and probably irrelevant. But an accumulation of them is doing so. Such exhibitions must be attempted — but with the clear realization that they may fail.

SATURDAY, AUGUST 24, 12:00 NOON

Session Leader:

STEVEN DURLAND

Topic:

CULTURE AND SOCIETY

Location:

CARE WORLD HEADQUARTERS, 151 ELLIS STREET NE

The humanitarian organization that was the site of this conversation has provided and continues to provide for the basic needs of people in developing countries and during war. The "CARE box," first distributed in 1946, is remembered by Europeans who lived through World War II .

Method of Preparation:

TAKE-OUT

On day four the food underlined America's multicutural society. The guests were free to choose take-out food; a kind of display of tastes and cultures resulted in the presentation of various dishes, from Asian to Mexican to Soul, each in a box. On the walls inside this building are photographs of people from around the world who receive CARE boxes. In the boardroom, where the conversation took place, each guest found the take-out box they had ordered. By contrast, the table setting was complete (with glassware, ceramic plates, flatware, and linens). The dessert was from Italian culture, a very special treat that one allows oneself only rarely.

Menu:

PROSECCO PRIMO FRANCO

TAKE-OUT ORDERED BY THE GUESTS

CAFFE CON LA PANNA

GRAPPA

STEVEN DURLAND

LOOKING FOR ART IN THE PROCESS

I'm groping for a way to start this essay. I keep wanting to say that last fall while in Atlanta I saw an artwork called *Brothers for Others: Sports, Surrogacy, and Society* by visual artist Maurice O'Connell. But in truth I didn't. I did go to Atlanta and visit the presentation venue. I did see the artist and talk with him at length. I read some short essays on his intentions for *Brothers* and some documentation on the creative process as it had progressed. But I didn't see the art.

O'Connell, like a number of visual artists today, is attempting to create what Joseph Beuys described as "social sculpture." For Beuys this meant applying the artist's prerogative of creative problem solving to the task of finding answers to social ills. The artist in me cringes even as I write that because of the enormity of all it implies.

Beuys's proposition is much more demanding than the political art that's so familiar today. Certainly there's a value in art that critiques society. Such art is a vital component of a cultural democracy and, at its finest, can have significant impact on the way we view the world. But relatively speaking, the artist who only critiques the ills of society is swimming in the shallow end of the pool with a life preserver on, compared to the artist who is trying to actively address those ills.[1]

Why? Because the social sculptor has set himself the task of directly intervening in people's lives. This is no small ambition and one that guarantees consequences, either positive or negative. A bad social sculpture has far greater consequences than a bad painting. You don't mess with people's lives and then just paint over it if it doesn't work.

Brothers for Others (BFO) documents O'Connell's efforts over a four-month residency to observe and investigate the dynamics of the Atlanta-area Boys & Girls Club. He believed that the resulting insights might be beneficial to those who had allowed him to witness their activities. He also thought those insights might be instructive for himself, since his ongoing art activity in Dublin is heavily invested in working with youth. Defined as such, *BFO* was, for all practical purposes, impossible to observe.

[1] It is important to point out that the body of work of any individual artist who is attempting to address social concerns rarely breaks down neatly into one or the other of these two categories. Rather it is quite common to find both kinds of work represented as the artist moves back and forth between a studio practice and a public practice, each feeding the other.

STEVEN DURLAND is a visual artist, writer, editor, and arts administrator. In 1995 he co-founded Art in the Public Interest (API), a nonprofit organization dedicated to the need for information about culturally engaged art. He has served as editor of the quarterly arts magazine *High Performance* since 1986, which in 1994 was awarded the Alternative Press Award for cultural coverage.

He has taught performance at the University of California, Irvine; served as a consultant in arts and marketing to the country of El Salvador; and spent two years working in the South Dakota Arts Council's artists-in-residence program. Since 1985 he has been a presenter and panelist at various conferences, universities, and arts organizations in the United States, Canada, and Europe. His work

as a visual artist has been presented around the United States and in Ireland. His writing frequently appears in *High Performance* as well as other magazines and catalogues. His essays have appeared in *Cultural Wars: Documents from the Recent Controversies in the Arts* (New Press, 1992) and *Art in the Public Interest* (UMI Press, 1989).

The fact that a work of art exists in such a way that it defeats viewer expectations or is totally resistant to viewing is not particularly unique. It was a frequent strategy of conceptual artists. But in this particular case it was not an intentional aesthetic construction but a basic fact of the work itself. For O'Connell, the art in *BFO* resides partly in the interaction that existed between himself and those inside the Boys & Girls Club who allowed his participation and partly in the results of that interaction. It is not just his experience with the club, but also the club's experience with him. It is not just the results of his experience but the results of their experiences. So the artwork as a whole is defined by multiple experiences of the process and multiple interpretations of the results. If O'Connell were to attempt to represent *BFO* as an artwork outside of the artwork itself (i.e., in a gallery or exhibition space), he would violate the basic integrity of his own artwork.

That is not to say that O'Connell can't present documentation of his activities in *BFO*; he has, but at some risk.[2] Regardless of O'Connell's sense of his role in the work, viewers of the documentation (when it is presented in an exhibition context) are likely to ascribe levels of authorship and autonomy to O'Connell that deny the multiple experiences and results.

So an appropriate "viewing" becomes further complicated by the fact that O'Connell did *BFO* as part of an exhibition in which he accepted funds from an arts institution to create a project inside a community where he was both literally and figuratively a foreigner. Such a situation can easily be seen as ethically questionable and perhaps downright colonial. O'Connell seems to have appreciated the contradictions this presented, and it's interesting to observe how he dealt with them both as an artist initiating involvement with a community and as an artist presenting an exhibition.

In defining his participation with the Boys & Girls Club, O'Connell limited his involvement to little more than observation. He notes, "I used this environment to explore and not necessarily to be useful or an asset." By avoiding the posture of an artist brought in to do something, he was searching for a way to sidestep expectations of an artist-audience hierarchy. The subtlety of O'Connell's concerns might get lost here. But as is reflected in his previous work, his goal is to work among a community, not with or for the community. In refusing to assert his role as artist during a short-term residency in an unfamiliar community, he in essence was allowing the community to make any determinations as to how he might be most valuable. He recognized that he was the "foreigner" and it was not his place to decide what was best for the community.

In defining his participation in "Conversations at The Castle," O'Connell tacitly reinforced this respect for the community's relationship in his work by making no effort to represent the community or the process in which he was participating with them. He merely made himself available to talk with visitors and provided texts describing an overview of the project. It became clear that he was questioning the role of the institution and the exhibition process in the kind of work he had defined for himself. And it also seems clear that while he's skeptical, he's not sure what the answer is yet.

All of which is to say that I didn't see the "art" in *Brothers for Others*. In fact, O'Connell is telling me I can't see the art, because it happens in a shared, participatory space defined by the artist and the community. It involves process and it produces a product and results, but if you're not a participant, you probably can't have a valuable sense of either.

2
There were display aspects of O'Connell's "research" materials, as he called them, at the Youth Art Connection Gallery and in his "office" at The Castle during the last phase of his project.

144

Durland

THE CHIMERICAL DILEMMAS

Today art like Maurice O'Connell's is often referred to as "community-based art," a term that is somewhat lacking in definitional rigor but does come closer than the term "social sculpture" to recognizing the actual dynamic of the artistic process. Social sculpture tends to imply that the artist is an external force imposing his or her creative will on a social situation and viewing the public as a medium to be manipulated. Such a view might better suit existing conventions for exhibition and critical analysis, but it is the antithesis of the successfully realized community-based artwork.

The community-based artist becomes an internal participant in the social situation. To quote Don Adams and Arlene Goldbard (who use the term "neighborhood artist"): "A neighborhood artist is someone whose work consists of placing artistic skills at the service of a community (neighborhood art thus also requires the skills of a community organizer — the ability to explain, assist, and learn from others). He or she abandons the old idea of the artist as a person who is set apart from others."[3]

So for the community-based artist, public reaction is not an after-the-fact acknowledgment of the artwork but a part of the creative process. Thus the actual artwork is formed through the quality of that interaction and might only be observed as the result of that interaction.

This becomes a dilemma for anyone trying to fit community-based work into art world conventions. First, it becomes art that is resistant to exhibition. That is not to say that a community-based art project might not result in art objects created by the artist (influenced by the community) or the community (influenced by the artist). Nor is it to suggest that those art objects lack artistic validity. Rather, it is to say that art objects are a by-product of the community-based artwork and need not exist for that artwork to be successful.

A prominent example is the work of Tim Rollins and K.O.S. (Kids of Survival). That Rollins's work with inner-city youth results in a number of museum-quality paintings is quite remarkable, yet the essence of this particular collaboration exists not in the paintings but in the impact of the artistic process on both the youth and the artist. The work of K.O.S. changed the lives of some of its participants, inspiring confidence and providing opportunities where there was little hope before. From a gallery or museum standpoint, that impact can at best exist as a contextual element to the paintings themselves.

Secondly, this work becomes resistant to conventional critical analysis. The critic can assume a role as observer, but it's problematic, perhaps even impossible, to presume the role of critic from a position outside the community where the work exists. Once the artist has become an internal participant, the role of critic falls to those who also participate internally. If the youth who participate in K.O.S., their parents, or their neighbors were to voice significant objection to Rollins's efforts, it would be presumptuous of any critic to suggest otherwise, no matter how elegant we might consider the project. As artist and arts administrator Bill Cleveland notes: "In all my years working with kids, prisoners, seniors, revolutionaries, and homeless folks never once did they ask

3
Don Adams and Arlene Goldbard, "Grassroots Vanguard," *Art in America* 70, 4 (April 1982): 23.

145

4
From an unpublished
e-mail conversation with
Bill Cleveland, 1996.

whether what we were doing was high, middle, or, God forbid, community art. They did let us know when they thought we were bullshitting though." [4]

This is not to say that there's no role for the outside observer, but conventional critical analysis changes to something more akin to cultural journalism. We can document what a community-based artwork has accomplished and examine the developments that led to that accomplishment. If the participating community views the artwork as successful, we can analyze the reasons it succeeded.

My writing about O'Connell's work above might be considered a critical response to the work. I would be hesitant to give that impression since for all practical purposes it ignores the artwork entirely to focus on O'Connell's artistic strategies. To call it critical analysis would be doing exactly what O'Connell fears — ascribing one-sided authorship to the work.

These dilemmas of exhibition and critical analysis have fostered a certain degree of antagonism toward community-based art in some circles. The fact of its resistance to conventions is perceived as a threat. And the antagonism manifests itself in the same manner it always has in the art world when new ideas threaten conventional wisdom. Defenders of the faith attack or studiously ignore the work. Practitioners and apologists for the last "new" idea develop a fear of finding themselves labeled mainstream and therefore irrelevant in an art world that promotes a hierarchy of innovation.

But such fears are overblown. Community-based art is not being practiced in opposition to conventional art practices but is rather a valuable extension of those practices. The artists who invest their creative energy in communities are applying much the same skills they practice in the studio and, generally speaking, these artists share their time doing both. In fact, it is precisely because these artists bring the skills and idealism of artmaking to bear on this work that it has impact and exists as art, not just as social work as some would derisively claim.

If we want to talk about this as a new avant-garde art movement (problematic as that idea might be), then it's possible to say it's the first such movement that doesn't challenge the art that has gone before it but rather champions art's intensified application in society. Community-based art has not departed from the conventions of art, but rather from the conventions of the arts infrastructure. That people on both sides of the issue have at times become defensive arises from a failure to recognize a shared commitment to the value of art in our culture.

The success of community-based art will speak well for the power of art in general and on a practical level help raise artistic literacy in a public that is often sorely lacking in even a rudimentary aesthetic vocabulary. After all, a public that has once again learned to appreciate art will support it both philosophically and financially.

THE ARTIST AS SELF-INTERESTED PARTICIPANT

The driving force behind community-based art and its departure from the arts infrastructure resides in the efforts of the artists who practice it. Some artists come to it through cultural tradi-

146

Durland

tion, others through a sense of political imperative. For some it's developed from following the more radical directions art has taken over the past forty years — happenings, conceptual art, performance art, and so on. Often artists become involved in community projects for no loftier motivations than because they offer opportunities when no others are present, finding themselves surprised to discover a fertile and rewarding way to practice art.

Maurice O'Connell noted that his experience in art school was alienating and didn't seem to fit with the way he wanted to practice art in the world. What he eventually discovered was a way of working that allowed him to invest his art skills in his concerns beyond the arts. Most artists search for that synergy. For some it means painting landscapes; for O'Connell it means working with youth and education programs.

Critics who want to dismiss community-based art as "social work" miss the boat entirely because they fail to perceive the artist's own selfish interest in doing this kind of work. Adams and Goldbard note, "Justification and gratification are inherent in neighborhood art; they are not postponed until the verdict of arbiters of success is given. Neighborhood artists want their work to have impact, to have meaning to others. Each day they are able to see that art can help transform the experience of the members of a community. Their work is thus not the expression of a single sensibility, but part of a continuing dialogue among the members of a community."[5]

In an interview I did with Grady Hillman, an established Texas poet who has worked in correctional institutions for many years, he said: "Working in the free world — writing poems, going the artist path, publishing in magazines, talking to other artists — was about craft more than anything else. And then I started working with inmates, for whom the creation of a poem was the most important thing in their life. They showed me how powerful a thing I'd latched onto, that I was working with something that was dangerous and explosive and intense and wonderful and magical, and that was good for me."[6]

Justification and gratification exist for artists in the conventional arts infrastructure, but they can be both rare and capricious. The high idealism characteristic of artists can find itself at odds with a support structure that rewards marketing, public relations, and salesmanship. These artists often discover that direct involvement with a community can validate their creativity and fulfill the need for self-expression.

Stuart Pimsler is a well-known choreographer who has begun working with health-care professionals, doctors, and nurses who daily face death and dying. Through the process of creating dance, they express their feelings about the burden of grief and loss. "There's a hunger [for these health-care professionals] to get to the core," says Pimsler, and he provides the artistic expertise. The process is undeniably therapeutic, and the product is acclaimed by the public as quality performance. For Pimsler, the work fulfills his core desire for intimacy in his artwork, an outcome he was unable to achieve with his own company of professional dancers. The process is so satisfying to all concerned that he says he may never return to working exclusively with professional artists.

When a method of artmaking is so satisfying to both artists and the public, it deserves our

5
Adams and Goldbard, "Grassroots Vanguard," 23.

6
Steven Durland, "Maintaining Humanity: Grady Hillman talks about arts programs in correctional settings," *High Performance* 19, 1 (Spring 1996):12.

attention as a viable and valuable practice. Yet I don't want to suggest that all artists move in this direction any more than I would suggest that all artists should be bronze sculptors. Like any art discipline, community-based art requires certain skills that not all of us possess or even have the ability or desire to learn. Unlike other mediums, it's probably a bit more important to discourage those who lack the necessary skills.

In the case of Christo, it is frequently pointed out that his work is heavily dependent on his ability to maneuver through multiple layers of public and private bureaucracy before he finally realizes his work. Similarly, for the community-based artist the ability to handle social negotiations and to treat cultural imperatives with sensitivity are not just personality traits but artistic skills necessary to realize an artwork.

Contrary to some opinions, community-based art is not a place for artists who are less skilled in traditional media. As Bill Cleveland pointed out, communities quickly perceive "bullshit." They expect talent and credentials in their artists, just as they do in their doctors and lawyers. Grady Hillman noted: "They see you as a model. They want a professional standard."

THE COMMUNITY AS SELF-INTERESTED PARTICIPANT

One of the side effects of community-based art has been a recognition of its impact on communities. Lately there have been many attempts to "quantify" the benefits of the arts so as to make them more appealing to the bottom-line oriented bureaucrats who are often asked to fund such projects. Recent studies have shown that participation in the arts can improve school test scores, reduce dropout rates, lessen crime rates, reduce the recidivism rates of inmates, contribute to mental and physical health, and create economic opportunity. Perhaps it's all true, and if it provides support for community-based art, so much the better. But I myself consider these statistics to be the by-products that result when people become actively involved in the creation of their own culture.

Too often our individual, community, and regional identities get lost in a world of mass culture. When our culture is defined for us by franchised stores, television, movies, large-circulation magazines, top-forty radio, major museums, concert halls, and best-seller lists, then we all live in a virtual city that's part Manhattan and part Hollywood. When most people walk out the door each morning, the world they see is of no consequence to the culture they live in. Their life stories and community histories are meaningless, except when they mirror the virtual culture that has been created for them.

All of which is leading me to say that it's not hyperbole to suggest that art, when applied at the community level, can be a powerful tool for re-establishing individual and community identity through a process that acknowledges the existence and fosters the development of local culture. It's a splendid and logical role for art, given that it is so poorly suited for the creation of mass culture. Whether we're talking about painting or dance, theater or poetry, we're talking about something that is intimate in its scale and ability to accommodate an audience. This intimacy is tacit permission for artists (whether trained professionals or amateurs inspired by the presence of a professional) to deal with the specifics of the immediate world around them. It is this intimacy that gives a voice to a local culture for a local culture. And if, in the course of addressing the specifics of a local culture, the artist also happens upon universal themes that can move a nation or a planet, then we'll always have a rationale for major museums.

Culture and Society — Guest List

Steven Durland, Editor, *High Performance*, North Carolina — Session Leader

Susan Bishop, Chaplain, Metro Correctional Instititution, Atlanta

Michael Brenson, critic, New York

Linda Burnham, Editor, *High Performance*, North Carolina

Ery Camara, artist, Mexico City

Mauricio Dias, artist, Basel

Amina Dickerson, Director, Corporate Contributions, Kraft Foods Foundation, Chicago

Darija Djavanovic, Save the Children, Clarkston Refugee Community Center, Atlanta

Gwendolyn Driscoll, Press Officer, CARE World Headquarters, Atlanta

Gail King Griffin, teacher, Atlanta

Kojo Griffin, artist, Atlanta

LaVone Griffin, Theatrical Visionaries, Atlanta

Anna Harding, Course Director, Visual Arts Department, Goldsmiths College, University of London

Glenn Harper, Editor, *Sculpture Magazine*, Washington, D.C.

Mary Jane Jacob, Curator, "Conversations at The Castle"

Jeffrey Kastner, Associate Editor, *ArtNews*, New York

David Levi-Strauss, critic, New York

Elizabeth MacGregor, Director, IKON Gallery, Birmingham, England

Stefania Mantovani, artist, artway of thinking, Venice

Anne Morgan, critic, Gainesville, Florida

Walter Riedweg, artist, Basel

Federica Thiene, artist, artway of thinking, Venice

Tricia Ward, Executive and Artistic Director, ARTScorpsLA, Los Angeles

SUNDAY, AUGUST 25, 6:00 P.M.

Session Leaders:

AMINA DICKERSON & TRICIA WARD

Topic:

YOUTH, ART, AND SOCIETY

Location:

YOUTH ART CONNECTION GALLERY

An exhibition space dedicated to showing work by, for, and about youth, this gallery seeks to forge links between youth and society through art. It is sited in downtown Atlanta along historic Auburn Avenue — the birthplace and resting place of Dr. Marin Luther King, Jr., and site of his church — and next door to the executive offices of United Way, the parent organization of the Boys and Girls Clubs.

Method of Preparation:

P-ASSAGGI

The menu was realized in collaboration with four youth participants. The tastes of one generation were offered to another, becoming a means of communication and expression, of giving and receiving. The students worked with the chef in the preparation of the food and they decided how to set the table. Food and drinks were placed in the center of the conversation table and served family style. The youth also participated in the conversation.

Menu:

LASAGNE WITH TOMATO SAUCE

PIZZA WITH ONIONS, MUSHROOMS, GREEN PEPPERS, SAUSAGE, FOUR CHEESES OR PINEAPPLE

GREEN SALAD WITH BLUE CHEESE DRESSING

GARLIC BREAD

VANILLA ICE CREAM AND SPRITE FLOATS

FRUIT PUNCH

CHOCOLATE ICE-CREAM CAKE WITH WHIPPED CREAM AND STRAWBERRIES

AMINA DICKERSON AND TRICIA WARD

A CO-MEDITATION ON YOUTH, ART, AND SOCIETY

AMINA: I was pleased to know that I'd be working with you, Tricia, although I'd never met you or, frankly, heard about your work. But I felt that the differences as well as the similarities in our work would make for an interesting collaboration as co-moderators for the "Conversations on Culture" session on youth, art, and society. Although we have both worked with youth intensively, our efforts have been shaped by different circumstances and perspectives. As a museum educator for twenty years, I've sought to enhance the range and quality of museum learning experiences. Though most children encounter museums via the yellow school bus, my work extends into classrooms, special summer programs, and, more significantly, teaching children on their own turf through outreach initiatives. Museum education departments have really pushed the margins of public engagement for museums, forcing them to examine all sorts of questions about access, the composition of audiences, and the experiences we create for visitors.

My museum work has always been informed by my earlier experience in improvisational theater with an acting troupe concerned primarily with the creative lives of young people, especially those in difficult social or emotional circumstances. These encounters made me a witness to

AMINA DICKERSON is director of corporate contributions at Kraft Foods Foundation, Chicago. Her work spans museums, arts and education, institutional development, and community-based arts collaborations. Recently a distinguished visitor at the John D. and Catherine T. MacArthur Foundation, she is a fellow at the Newberry Library. From 1989 to 1996 she was director of education and later vice president for education and public programs at the Chicago Historical Society. Previous posts include president of Chicago's DuSable Museum of African American History; assistant executive director of Philadelphia's Afro-American Historical and Cultural Museum; program director for the Smithsonian's National Museum of African Art; and community relations director for the Living Stage Improvisational Theater Company at Arena Stage, Washington, D.C. She regularly serves as a panelist and consultant to foundations; speaks at museums, professional associations, and arts organizations; and serves on the boards of the National Postal History Museum, the Children and Family Justice Center, and the African American Museums Association. She holds an MA in arts management from the American University, studied theater arts at Emerson College, Boston, and holds a certificate from the Harvard University Program in Arts Administration.

TRICIA WARD has created public and private sculptural environments and taught multidisciplinary arts. In the mid-1980s she began to explore the concepts of park and art as one entity. She has furthered her investigations with an analysis of public policy in relation to urban land use, setting in motion a move toward using private land for more public functions. Since 1992 she and hundreds of young people have created *La Tierra de la Culebra* (The Land of the Serpent), a community youth art park that acts as a living laboratory for experimental learning through a multitude of interdisciplinary activities for its community members — from young children through graduate students. Out of this collaborative effort, Ward founded ARTScorpsLA, a public art organization dedicated to teaching life skills through the arts. As its artistic and executive director, Ward works with communities to transform vacant land into vital public places. ARTScorpsLA's neighborhood revitalization goals include: improving streetscapes and Los Angeles public schools, encouraging the prevention of graffiti, and creating murals and sculptural environments. Ward was recently appointed the arts commissioner to the City of Los Angeles Commission on Children, Youth and Their Families.

art's power to enable young people to express their world views, hopes, and aspirations. With each encounter with art and artists, their experiences evolved. Art gave their ideas form and validation. When young people recognize art's possibilities and its potential for self-expression, they continue to seek opportunities to experiment with all forms of artmaking.

TRICIA: For twenty-five years I have created public and private sculptural environments using the earth as my palette. I felt compelled through my site-specific work, which represents and reclaims nature's organic process, to undo the damage humans have done to the environment.

In the studio, I created sculptural and two-dimensional objects that addressed social and political conditions of concern to me. At the same time I taught photography, sculpture, printmaking, ceramics, and mural painting to elementary- through college-level students, incorporating those same ideas.

It became apparent to me that the parts of my professional life — site-specific work, the creation of smaller objects, and teaching — were related and could benefit by coming together in an integrated way. I felt that a single, multifaceted combination would reflect more cogently the possibilities of art as a powerful vehicle for the cultivation of a healthy humanity.

From 1987 to 1989, I orchestrated a community reclamation of a turn-of-the-century park in New York City's Lower East Side, to create an artful environment — an oasis within the harsh surrounding neighborhood. The stark transformation this hands-on activity created made me realize the potential for making a real difference and made me feel that in this situation I was using myself fully as an artist.

Shortly after the 1992 riots in Los Angeles, I joined other artists who were asked to initiate community arts workshops for youth to help develop the potential role of the arts in healing social and community problems. Rather than create a short-lived workshop as a temporary Band-Aid for dealing with the deep social problems evident, I chose to place a fertility symbol, representing the growth and future of our youth, on a piece of fallow land to create a sense of place and a platform for the unrequited voices of young people. This two-acre urban community art park, *La Tierra de la Culebra* (The Land of the Serpent), has as its centerpiece a 500-foot "serpent" made from tiles, stones, and rubble unearthed on the lot, which I constructed with the help of community young people over a period of several years. We also terraced and cultivated the landscape, fulfilling the objectives of artful ownership and cogent pride. This is how I find myself — teaching children, teenagers, and young adults life skills through the arts, while I myself become a student of the streets.

AMINA: In Atlanta, you'll recall we had three teens help prepare our meal and then join us at the table. They were very forthcoming about their views and opinions, seeking to help a rather disparate group of adults understand, even fleetingly, the reality of their world. I believe your work with urban youth has a natural link to their experiences, and I am inspired to think about the ways in which museums might more effectively connect to both the creative spirit and the personal struggles faced by most teens today.

Dickerson and Ward

TRICIA: I felt there was a tremendous value in having youth at the conversation who could express to us the daily reality of violence in their lives and on the streets. But I regretted that the professionals at the table did not pursue further conversation about these realities. Rather, they considered their concerns — their projects, curricula development, effective strategies for working with youth — more valid points for exploration. Though stimulated, I simultaneously struggled with myself about these issues. A void remained.

AMINA: Yes, the comments of the teens sent me into a personal reverie as well. How different our opportunities! We had options; we came to art with multiple vehicles for expression. Though they clearly identified the ways in which they express themselves or make art ("in the way we dress," one replied), the access to artistic media seems much more constrained. I recalled my earliest awareness of the extraordinary power of art, the liberating experience of writing poetry, dancing, performing. It allowed me tools of communication — to peers, to parents, to the larger world.

TRICIA: The majority of neighborhoods in Los Angeles are densely populated with diverse immigrant communities. On average, fifty percent of those living in these neighborhoods are young people under the age of eighteen with up to thirty-eight percent living below the poverty line. The public schools do not offer arts education at any level. Thus, the creation of modes of artistic expression must come from within the young people themselves. As I expose young people to art techniques and histories, they devour it and then incorporate their newfound knowledge into their personal and societal realities. They do not depart from their personal dialogue; they expand upon it. So, I feel it is a matter of exposure, resources, and quality of experience with the arts, which young people are so deserving of, that will give them the tools to communicate within their communities and with the world at large.

As we talk, three key words keep coming to mind. If we could locate a conversation about youth and society, I think these words embody it all. The concept of conversation and the level of communication this implies; place, where art is formally sited, where it miraculously appears, where we hold conversations, and where there is an opening for communication; and longevity, perhaps the most important quality, which is the outgrowth of the success of the first two.

AMINA: The impetus for the Atlanta conversation was art and our shared belief in its transformative and communicative possibilities. But art's vocabulary is dynamic, ever-changing. The brief conversation at the table with the teens amplified this point: "It is in our music, it is in the way we dress, the language we use with each other. This is our art." The art of youth today remains distinctive, a window on its time and place. For example, I look at hip hop culture as an honest expression of its time. Its message transcends race and geography as witnessed by Japanese, Chinese, and French rappers. It's very interesting to me that having carved out its own stylized place, its impact is now so pervasive as to be co-opted by the marketing machine. Like other art forms, the power of hip hop has been subverted in order to sell it to youth worldwide. In this context, art created the

153

possibility of an international community, but external forces then exploited the original truth of the art. While such uses of art are not confined to commercial distribution, the "edge" of the artwork or expression has been changed and its power diminished.

TRICIA: Funny you should use that word, because I was particularly disturbed in Atlanta by the casual use of the word "community." If you look in the dictionary at all the words starting with "commun," the first is "communal." Reading through the list of words derived or related to community, all speak to a form of shared interest in communication, ownership of place, and commitment. Over dinner, many of the art administrators, critics, social workers, social organization administrators, and artists opined that educators were responsible for the deteriorating relationship between youth and their communities. Educators were described as linear thinkers, often too structured to be responsive to the ideas and voices of youth. Yet, many educators provide a natural point of intersection through which we can and should build community. Rather than indict educators for their lack of innovation, we should acknowledge that they, too, are searching for resolution and are an integral part of their "community."

I focus on the idea of community because it is young people who really define it. They share in the creation of art as life, as manifested by their creative talk, walk, clothing, painting, and music. The loudness of color, form, and hardness of edge is a reaction to and rejection of the established method of expression. Really, it seems that many of this generation of young people are far more grounded in their rejection of societal norms than my generation was. This is partially because of a reaction to and a rejection of the most recent decade: the "me generation." They seem more soulful and engaged in a development of equity, which sometimes takes a separatist stance as implied in "ethnic nationalism" yet often has and can have the goal of achieving parity for all. Their awareness of and even emphasis on "multiculturalism" is partly a reaction to their strikingly different posture on personal identity.

AMINA: But aren't their generational responses to "mainstream society" influenced in some unconscious way by the traditions of protest and personal freedom that preceded them? Don't we all consciously or unconsciously both build upon and react to the cultural norms that preceded us?

TRICIA: Absolutely! The rejection but at the same time unaffected incorporation of precedent is a natural evolution. But, in my experience, there does seem to be a current loud rejection of self-interest. Today's youth were dramatically influenced by the Reagan and Bush eras and witnessed the dramatic and ever more alarming divide between the "haves and have-nots." Because of this, perhaps it has become more important to these young people to become better citizens of the community. Furthermore, their imaginations are spurred by accelerated information sources, while they live every day with the knowledge that they can be killed at any moment, for no reason. Similar values are also evident in the USC graduate students who assist in the administration and programming at ARTScorpsLA. I have witnessed them reject the academic precedent and careers in more traditional "public art" organizations to work within what they consider a more satisfying grass-roots structure where they have a more hands-on commitment.

AMINA: I was also struck by the comments of the young brother Darryl about the violence he felt he faced everyday. It echoed the daily violence faced by other young people with whom we've worked. Their generation seems marked by escalating brutality, and, though it is our larger society that has created this environment for them, we seem repelled by their ability to cope. We penalize and denigrate them for their attitudes about violence, for their apparent comfort with guns and death. Yet, it is our adult society that has shaped much of their world and the images that assault them — in the media, on television, even in personal interactions across the great racial divide. So perhaps we shouldn't be surprised by the fact that violence seems to characterize so much of their world, their music, their social affiliations, their language. At the conversation table this young man offered us his profoundly tragic reality in describing the appearances he assumes on the street to survive day by day. He girds himself and internalizes not only his fear and pain but his dreams and aspirations as well.

TRICIA: I believe this internalization has its parallel in people who have directly experienced war. They develop a capacity to insulate and to endure, which are both economic and psychological requirements of the situation. Youth live this as they are faced with the absence of dreams and a future. They allow violence, as an emblematic image of immortality, to represent their power, which may be the only aspiration they recognize as attainable. That is why art can be so powerful for these youths. It is an alternative means of personal self-expression that is directly attainable. One of the problems we encounter, though, is that many young people feel they have "no time!" We are competing with the "fast bucks" of the streets, immediate and tangible gratification that unfortunately reflects the hastened environment that engulfs the lives of youth today.

AMINA: Art could provide, should provide, opportunities to make meaning of this existence, to respond to and reform it. Perhaps if we better understood the internalized responses of youth to this environment, we could serve them. But it requires a sustained dialogue that is informed at its core by the capacity of art to transcend and transform a present reality, to express aspirations, desires, and fears.

TRICIA: Obviously art cannot and will not touch or alter the lives of all youth. But many more can be embraced and engaged if we give ourselves to them as artists, role models, friends, and teachers.

AMINA: The grounding of our creative endeavor would move from being reactive. Our fear of our children would dissipate. The function of art in their lives — and ours — could be forthrightly proactive and life-centered and could play a role in overturning a life defined by the presence of death.

TRICIA: The violence in our communities is often directly related to territory and borders, which is why the issue of place takes on particular significance. Whose place is it? The resolution is too frequently determined by violence. Lack of place is the cause. Too often in the low-income neighborhoods there is so little sense of ownership that simply traversing the territory of the streets can violate a contrived sense of ownership. Parents have confronted me with comments that their "community" is bordered by such-and-such a street and they do not want their youth beyond that line or other young people from outside to come within their borders. The significance of territory in economic terms is acutely understood on the street. Yes, we need an extended conversation allowing for the voices of all members of the community — youth, parents, educators, artists, museums, politicians, police, businesses, service providers, and whoever else feels the need for a voice — to work collectively on this issue of community building by confronting violence and the lack of communal trust.

Amina, you say we must be proactive. My creative process, coupled with that of the young people I have worked with for years, is to try and create a place of unity without a declaration of exclusion or reactionary implications, but at the same time a place where all views — positive and negative — are freely aired. Environmental sculpting of the urban landscape provides an arena in which the purest possible form of democracy can take shape and grow. This system also engages the assets of each individual, develops self-expression, communication, cooperative learning skills, and the tools necessary to work in close collaboration with others. The children and young adults learn conflict resolution through open discussion forums. The surrounding community is inherently part of the collaboration of communication at *La Tierra de la Culebra*. This model and the lessons learned from it can be used at multiple sites, each one of which will provide new lessons and experiences that can help us use this form as a vehicle of social change.

AMINA: I wish more museums would pursue that kind of approach! Unfortunately, today's youth don't feel particularly welcome in museums. Aside from episodic programs and a new trend for teen docents, they are largely excluded. The institutional culture of our museums affirms solitude, order. We lack staff, resources, and the will to address effectively the culture or the needs of young adults. We are certainly not alone in this stance, for youth soon discover there are few places that welcome them. But this doesn't absolve us of our obligation to serve young people. Youth culture emerged with a vengeance in the 1950s — and with it a plethora of places devoted to the needs of youth culture. Today, it is on the streets and in the malls that youth make places for themselves.

TRICIA: Exactly. "Kickin it" (in street lingo) is a healthy and historical pursuit. It's a natural socialization process fulfilling a need to gather together, to commune, to develop language and dialogue, and to create and declare self, particularly in relation to others.

Amina, you commented on the lack of staff and resources and, importantly, an absence of willingness to address youth culture. First, you must consider whether youth want a relationship with the museum. Understand that it is possible that rejection of the museum is linked with disdain for the mainstream. So, if artists and museums want to work with the youth of the streets they must be willing to relinquish some of their academic approaches and structures and to access and respect a newly established paradigm of expression. Artists and museums must collaborate to create an alliance with youth, one appealing to their desires and needs.

AMINA: I believe today we have a number of museum models that operate outside preconceived "mainstream" notions and perhaps are poorly served by the "museum" moniker. But preconceptions can only be changed through sustained communication. Which brings me to the concern for longevity. You've mentioned you no longer do projects, which struck a particular chord in me. I've thought about "projects" recently as I struggled with my own frustration and guilt for efforts that could not be sustained within my museum work. Projects have merit within the constellation of museum activities and do have impact, though it is sometimes difficult to determine exactly how the fleeting exposure, the brief discussion, the forty minutes of hands-on experience can have lasting value. Nonetheless, studies show that students often remember a magical moment in a museum that provides the spark for a lifetime of study. For many, this is not enough, and interactions with art over time are what is needed to make a difference in their lives. And, as a colleague has pointed out, for far more young people there are no opportunities at all for the magical moment to take place, so distant is art from their lives.

I recall a five-month mentoring program that gave me a new understanding of the potential of museums to serve. Targeted to young African-American girls "at risk," this program revealed to me — and some 150 adult women — the profound need for us to be involved in their lives. I return often in my mind to the hunger for counsel and support I encountered in these young women. And yet, for all they did not bring, all they did not have, they gave their mentors a sense of purpose and a new way of seeing their own possibilities. But then it ended. And in bidding them farewell, my recognition of the limitations of working in museums became acutely apparent. Like so much else they experienced in life, we had let the girls down. We had started a deeply personal "conversation," which now would not — could not — be extended. With another exhibition on the way, it was the museum's time to move on. In countless ways the girls let us know that they not only came to feel at home in the museum but that they needed to continue their association. Formally, we could not. We did not.

So from this I resolved that as much as possible I would seek to create projects of longer duration, informed by my sense that projects in and of themselves are not enough. It is true that programs offering initial exposure and short-term efforts can have impact on the youth involved. But how much greater impact can we have when such programs are longer? The basic design of these projects must increasingly incorporate objectives and structures that will enable them to be sustained in some form over time — by the museum or cultural institution, by communities, or whenever possible through a collaboration among all. And this sentiment also was echoed around the table in Atlanta. Museums, schools, communities, artists — any of us endeavoring to create

157

Dickerson and Ward

a bond of trust and communication with youth — understand there must be a commitment of time. Longevity is instrumental in extending the efficacy of our work. More important, for those whose futures have been circumscribed to the margins, sustained programs and the communication, sharing, and collaboration they can yield will allow us to more fully and creatively serve youth and society.

TRICIA: Artists often come to me to do projects with the kids, expecting me to introduce and engage the youth in their ideas because I have an established relationship with them. I respond that in order for their projects to work, they themselves must first develop the trust and respect of those with whom they are working. I cannot do that for them, nor can I translate someone else's imagination and form of expression. This is too easy, self-serving, or exploitative, and a facile intent of exchange. Interestingly, when I state that I will not do their work for them they more often than not leave and go elsewhere. Their intent is a typical "parachute project" that fulfills something for the artist but not for the youth. The ultimate growth for these young people comes from the merging of youth's paradigm and the artists' learned paradigm, blended with knowledge of and from youth. Longevity ensures the formulation, over time, of new forms of communication and dialogue and thus creates this desired community intersection.

AMINA: I do want to affirm the importance of small efforts of short duration. These do have value, especially in the absence of other forms of engagement, as long as they are well-informed and grounded in an understanding and respect for youth. Unfortunately, we lack a balance in offerings. It's nearly always short-term.

TRICIA: For me, the value of the program you described was the personalization of exchange through which a dialogue intrinsic to the creation of a new community evolved, despite the brevity. The young girls left this experience with a sense of their own value and importance. One objective of mine is to blur the boundaries between audience and artist, artist and community; it translates to artist as citizen.

ARTScorpsLA's mission is "the linking of a healthy humanity to a healthy environment." I am very demanding on this point. I feel it is essential for artists to develop a conversation rather than a monologue. We must cultivate humanity while we toil the soil. Cultivating our food, we grow a new crop of cogent, conscious, and respectful humans to propel us into a vital, fertile, and bountiful future.

AMINA: From whatever place we come, it is critical that we commit ourselves to working across the art and social service divide, to forge strategies that truly serve young people.

TRICIA: Yes. Museums, artists — all of us working in the cultural realm — must become a community in order to create a more textural blend that will engage youth in substantive arts experiences.

Dickerson and Ward

Youth, Art, and Society — Guest List

Amina Dickerson, Director, Corporate Contributions, Kraft Foods Foundation, Chicago — Session Co-leader

Tricia Ward, Executive and Artistic Director, ARTScorpsLA, Los Angeles — Session Co-leader

Valerie Anderson, youth participant, Atlanta

Michael Brenson, critic, New York

Linda Burnham, Editor, *High Performance*, North Carolina

Bill Cleveland, Director of Education, Walker Art Center, Minneapolis

Rebecca DesMarais, Director, Youth Art Connection Gallery/ Boys & Girls Clubs of Metro Atlanta

Mauricio Dias, artist, Basel

Steve Durland, Editor, *High Performance*, North Carolina

Melanie Fernandez, Community Arts Development Officer, Ontario Arts Council, Toronto

Jennifer Friday, M.D., Centers for Disease Control, Atlanta

Mary Jane Jacob, Curator, "Conversations at The Castle"

Sylvia Jones, youth participant, Atlanta

Shantras Lakes, Outreach Coordinator, Department of Education, High Museum of Art, Atlanta

Karen Luik, Chair, Department of Education, High Museum of Art, Atlanta

Elizabeth MacGregor, Director, IKON Gallery, Birmingham, England

Stefania Mantovani, artist, artway of thinking, Venice

Darryl Mapp, youth participant, Atlanta

Maurice O'Connell, artist, Dublin

Walter Riedweg, artist, Basel

Charles Sessoms, artist, Atlanta

Pamela D. Sezgin, Director, Teaching Museum South, Fulton County Schools, Atlanta

Maureen Sherlock, critic, Chicago

Mary Ellen Strom, artist, New York

Felicia Taylor, Director, College Bound Program, Boys & Girls Clubs of Metro Atlanta

Federica Thiene, artist, artway of thinking, Venice

Jerry Tipton, Director, Boys & Girls Clubs of Metro Atlanta

Torreon Thompson, youth participant, Atlanta

WEDNESDAY, AUGUST 28, 6:00 P.M.

Session Leader:

SUSAN KRANE

Topic:

COMMUNICATIONS

Location:

AT&T, PROMENADE ONE LOBBY,
PEACHTREE AND FIFTEENTH STREETS NE

The southeast regional headquarters of the largest telecommunications company in the United States was the site of this conversation. However, in its architectural expression this office tower is mute and unrevealing of the high technology that AT&T represents. Only the lobby signage and banners hint at the company's operations.

Method of Preparation:

CONFEZIONATO

This evening we chose a typology of food: wrappers. The elements used to assemble this meal were on the table; from the various ingredients, the participants made their selections and placed them within the wrappers — closed casings that contained but also concealed the unique combinations of food. Even the dessert took the form of a wrapper food. This method underlined how when personal communications, specialized languages, or those of different cultures take on a technological or informational form, they also risk a loss of understanding.

Menu:

PROSECCO PRIMO FRANCO

INVOLTINI
DI FOGLIE DE VERZA
AI GAMBERETTI,
DI PROSCIUTTO,
DI FOGLIE DI CAVOLO ROSSO
ALLE VERDURE,
DI TACCHINO ALL'AVOGADO

PANZEROTTI

PITA CON LE PERE
E IL PROVOLONE

FRAGOLINO BIANCO

CANNOLI SICILIANI

ESPRESSO ILLY

GRAPPA

SUSAN KRANE

QUESTIONS FROM THE CASTLE

After years of working in mainstream museums, I was left with the distressing feeling that the mechanisms and machinations of institutions often had little to do with the realities of art, artist, and audience anymore — little to do with the private pleasure of seeing art carefully, over time, and little to do with the public satisfaction of community access and interchange. I now find myself located in the middle of the western United States, near the edge of the Continental Divide. The place seems more marginal than centered (unless you can appreciate the Zen-like quality of feeling equally far from everywhere else). The opportunity to converge in Atlanta for "Conversations on Culture" with colleagues similarly involved in the practice of presenting contemporary art was thus a welcome one. "Conversations at The Castle" offered a chance to assess alternatives and to look broadly at the state of the field as we approach the home stretch of the century. Where does contemporary art site itself in times that fluctuate between nostalgia and techno-futurism, greater affluence and greater limitations, diversification and mainstream encampment?

The three long evenings of "Conversations on Culture" I attended meandered wildly, as if infected by the unsettledness of working in professional territory that has shifted nervously for nearly a decade. Discussions were at times enlightening, at times beleaguered. No matter what the topic of the evening, participants (the majority of whom came of age professionally in the 1980s) seemed to be trying to thread a circuitous path between personal values and the circumstances of practice. Amid the din, it became comforting and clarifying — somewhat like watching TV with the mute button on — to look literally at where we were.

The Castle is an imposing granite masonry residence that survives in the midst of Atlanta's midtown forest of high-rises and condos, rescued from destruction by AT&T. It crowns a hill (of course), which once afforded a sense of social position as well as a view. Now it squats, usually vacant,

SUSAN KRANE is director of the University Art Galleries, University of Colorado at Boulder. From 1987 to 1995, she served as curator of modern and contemporary art at the High Museum in Atlanta; from 1979 to 1987 as curator at the Albright-Knox Art Gallery in Buffalo; and from 1978 to 1979 as Rockefeller Foundation fellow at the Walker Art Center, Minneapolis. Krane received a BA from Carleton College in Northfield, Minnesota, and an MA from Columbia University. Among the numerous exhibitions she has organized are "Tampering: Artists and Abstraction Today"; "Equal Rights and Justice" (a series of installations and public projects commemorating the civil rights movement); "Max Weber: The Cubist Decade, 1910-1920"; "Lynda Benglis: Dual Natures"; "Hollis Frampton: Recollections/Recreations"; and exhibitions and special projects by Mario Merz, General Idea, William Wegman, Judy Pfaff, Creighton Michael, Benny Andrews, Sherrie Levine, Houston Conwill, Ida Applebroog, Joel Otterson, Barbara Ess, Alison Saar, and Ray Smith. In addition to exhibition catalogues, she authored Albright-Knox Art Gallery — The Painting and Sculpture Collection, Acquisitions Since 1972 (Hudson Hills Press, 1987) and "Striking Out: Another American Road Show" in Scoring in Heaven (Aperture, 1991).

in the long shadows of its corporate neighbors. For the presentation of "Conversations at The Castle," the mansion was appended by a wooden entrance ramp that snaked alongside the building. This lengthy walkway extended The Castle's turf, providing a protective buffer for its end-of-the-century circumstances. The site had the imposing, willful look of a construction zone. The lexicon of words stenciled over the slatted sides of the rampway seemed to people this business-like place, warmly, by the simple virtue of conveying a poetic presence of mind where usually none is found. The language was suggestive and ambiguous, made more so by the fact that the letters were fragmented; you had to work a bit to see words in their entirety. Making one's way up the ramp required several pivots in direction. The indirect process of entering the space seemed a metaphor for the shifts and deadlocks we negotiate just to get to the starting gate of conversing about culture today.

To converse: to keep company with, to turn around, to exchange. The givens: an obsolete baronial mansion, physically overtaken by glass and steel skyscrapers, and buttressed by a renegade and purposefully makeshift postmodern entrance. Past private wealth and altruism. Corprorate business interests. Public interventions. These recombinant components are locations of cultural patronage. Who maintains our cultural houses these days? In an era of various continental and quantum shifts, can we presume to construct permanency? Can we incubate culture, or is it rather a process of transmission that we enact? How do these systems of power, support, and influence align themselves today? Which remain vital, which just linger on? How does each circumscribe audience and purpose? Does this intelligent, linguistic ramp represent a bridge between peoples and experiences or a fire escape for a site of practice torched by cultural retreat?

Nearby, just an intersection away, sits the High Museum of Art, the host of the Cultural Olympiad's showpiece extravaganza, "Rings: Five Passions in World Art." "Rings" and "Conversations at The Castle" are natural foils, barometers of opposite hemispheres of practice and opposite approaches to art, audience, and exhibition. Indeed, "Rings" was raised as a point of reference in every conversation I attended at The Castle and on the sidelines as well. (Since I previously worked at the High Museum, these lines of questioning hit particularly close to home.) Are the values represented here mutually exclusive, even oppositional? Does the present sense of dichotomy mean that we've come to a fork in roads that used to run parallel?

"Rings" was a decidedly linear experience, with a clear and nontransgressable traffic flow. It was a blockbuster show that conveyed overarching surety and authority, taken here to new ends. The experience of artwork — much of it fabulous — was highly mediated, categorized, even prescribed with emotional response (specifically: love, anguish, awe, triumph, joy). The art was uprooted from the cultures of its making and cast into a world of superlatives and aestheticization in place of historicity. The audience was given privileged access to masterpieces, prestige by virtue of proximity, and the fictive ability to move seamlessly across time, culture, and class. It was an exquisite, romanticized framework, one that was neutralized but not politically neutral by any stretch. "Rings" reflected an encompassing belief in universality, albeit self-defined. It deleted the need to muddle around in one's own complex psyche.

162

Krane

We live in an age of talk radio, talk shows, chat rooms, call-in TV, newspaper opinion polls on every subject, focus groups, and political platforms decided by test markets. Voices have been equalized, to the nth degree, creating lots of noise but rarely expertise or depth. Do people at heart crave a facade of surety? The assumption of authority? Absolute events, like "Rings," that construct consensus? Do we long for belonging, for times past and places far away, denuded of specificity and in effect "colorized" for us?

We have come to use audience as a means of validating cultural activities and measuring their "success." We owe this, in part, to the attacks on public funding of the arts and the need to justify government appropriations with quantifiable proof. Our focus on audience is also a result of institutions' quest for the earned income of the "gate" and of an ingrained, latter-day American trust in consumerism, like it or not. Perhaps the numbers bear out our interpretation of democracy, and a desire for widespread relevancy that contradicts the very notion of an avant-garde. As we struggle to measure effectiveness, numbers look good — real — given that responses to art are at heart abstract, cumulative, and not easily qualifiable or verbalized. When, however, does our focus on audience confuse the issue and lead us to mistake "market" for community, consumption for perception?

Community-based endeavors like "Conversations at The Castle" frequently involve groups of people who do not traditionally attend museums (here, visitors to a pedestrian-accessible temporary exhibition space, inmates in the detention system, youth in the Boys & Girls Club, residents of the African-American neighborhood of Reynoldstown, and the random person who entered via the Internet). They focus on process more than product, on the value of multiple voices, and on the irresolution and indeterminacy that exist in everyday life outside of institutional constructs. They strive not for monumentality or masterpiece status but for meaningful — and timely — personal involvement. They adopt the breadth and uncertainty of populism and at times the (problematic) mantle of social service. The discourse they take on verges on anthropology. These collaborative projects explore ways of re-rooting artmaking in the genuineness of "other" people's lives, given a society where mass culture is secularized and contemporary art has been widely denounced as elitist. At The Castle, art is a vehicle for individualized, embodied communication. Personal circumstances, class, identity, and ethnicity stay in the foreground.

Such projects are laboratories of practice — both social and artistic. They tend to spin off big questions and posit differences without whitewashing them. At the same time, they assume a political imperative by virtue of their radical pretext and by their subversion of hierarchies and the status quo. This can carry, as critic Hal Foster claims, "the danger, for the artist as ethnographer, of 'ideological patronage.'"[1] Inclusivity is tough terrain to negotiate, complicated by the fact that the initiative for participation is often imported from outside the designated community. It reflects, however, a search for meaning and for a realm of artistic possibility that remains unsatisfied and unnourished within the parameters of studio production or the conventions of institutional presentation. The number of people participating in these alternative endeavors or seeing the results may

1
Hal Foster, *The Return of the Real: The Avant-Garde at the End of the Century* (Cambridge, Massachusetts: The MIT Press, 1996), 173.

Krane

be relatively unimpressive and ultimately inconsequential to their "success."

In contrast, there is the mass popularity of "Rings," which visitors waited in long lines to see. While discussing the exhibition and its premise, I was accused by a friend (a political lobbyist) of elitism. Attendance figures were the true test of the exhibition's "democracy" for her: mass appeal became content. Yet "Rings" is a trophy show in which privilege is both capitalized on and shared, beneficently. Can "Rings" really simply be about the feat of bringing great art from around the world to the hinterlands and the opportunity granted to partake of it? (It's important to note that the show included only a few works by living artists. Its patina was one of timelessness not timeliness.) Who is this eager audience; what do they take away from this grandiose experience to their next expectation of art? "Rings" was perhaps perfectly matched to the international corporate context of the 1996 Olympics and inextricable from its marketing. The museum became the popular culture palace. The gritty, perhaps difficult art projects at The Castle stood, in contrast, like some Piranesian reminder of the poignancy of our ordinariness, labors, and mortality.

Nostalgia seems to come into play here on several levels — nostalgia for "culture" that is distant and esteemed, for a clarity that seems blissfully out of sync with the complexity of our times. When venturing beyond the walls of museums and locating contemporary art practice in a participatory, socially active realm, are we not also nostalgic for recovering a breadth of purpose; for art that speaks deeply to the specific circumstances of lives; for a sense of realism and connection that undercuts the superficial homogeneity of cultural consumerism? When we talk about "communities" is our purposefulness already an admission of a lack of belonging?

2
Nicholas Negroponte,
Being Digital (New York:
Vintage, 1995), 182.

Today, much of our information is delivered via electronic media. Experience is virtual as well as face-to-face. We communicate (transmit) as much or more than we commune. How can art function in a world where, as cyber guru Nicholas Negroponte forecasts, we've moved from atoms to bits as our primary basis of interaction?[2] Can either of these exhibition strategies — the macro blockbuster or the micro populist venue — address changes occurring in modes of community, perception, and learning, or address the fact that we are increasingly active agents rather than passive recipients of information? How will our readings of static objects — with their visceral, sensory effects and wonderfully insistent materiality — relate to this scenario? Our socializing experiences are no longer only rooted in time and place but are also based on nonlinear communications that may never involve real-time exchange. How will these realms relate? Where will we find, where will we feel, the acts of belonging? "Does communication take the place that culture used to?" asked Anne Balsamo in the conversation I moderated, which was about the potential of the Internet vis-à-vis artistic practice.

This conversation touched on several sensitive points of contention. At times, lines became drawn in the sand and attempts at exchange fell by the wayside. One of the participants called me afterward and lamented, "It was the worst dinner party I've ever been to." People squabbled from narrow points of view or from too-similar art world experiences. The talk and the adamancy revealed much about our habitualness, our insularity, and the professional identities in which we are deeply entrenched. Only occasionally did discussion hint at the potential for visionary thinking regarding the technology that stretches seductively in front of us, one of few open ranges on the horizon. For professionals who function beyond geographical boundaries as a matter of course, who time-shift and embrace abstractions with apparent ease, we were surprisingly far behind the curve. After all, the art community itself is a geographically dispersed network of colleagues who come face-to-face only periodically. It has in some respects been virtual for a long time, if safely self-contained.

Our conversation was held in the hermetic, glass-walled lobby of the AT&T building near The Castle, amid the courses of artway of thinking's dinner of rolled and wrapped foods (from cabbage leaves to cannoli). The stage was one of communion; the context was tied to the familial (which as Joyce Fernandes pointed out, also manifests itself as dysfunction and miscommunication). The discussion began, ironically, with Arturo Lindsay's disavowal of interest in the Internet, whose hype of globalism and democracy he denounced as a guise for elitism. Inequities of access were raised repeatedly and energetically during the evening, with several examples of Internet use in China, Africa, and Eastern Europe raised as counterpoints. (The fastest growth in on-line availability in 1994 was actually in Argentina, Iran, Peru, Egypt, Slovenia, the Philippines, the former Soviet Union, and Indonesia.) Sides were taken on this playing field from the beginning, with heated denial of exclusivity coming from Nicholas Drake, who used himself as an example of someone of limited means who is computer savvy and fully "wired." (He is dependent on public assistance due to health problems.) Anne Balsamo argued that the mythical "primitive" who doesn't want access to the Internet doesn't exist. Lindsay firmly retorted: "We're not talking about communication. We're talking about conversation with elite people."

This positioning reflected personal interest levels in and experience with technology as well as personal politics. Absenting oneself from the medium and its critical debate reinforces a place of marginality but also plays into the hands of the myth that relegates cultural ethnicity to grassroots expression (meaning technically unsophisticated or incapable). Guillermo Gomez-Peña's perspective on cyberspace and on his role as an "information superhighway bandido" is a useful point of reference and alterity. For Gomez-Peña, the positivist language of the Net and of technology feigns a "politically neutal/raceless/genderless/classless territory" that is as ethnocentric as ever. Gomez-Peña thus takes his position of "cultural invader": "What we want is to 'politicize' the debate: to 'brownify' virtual space; to 'spanglishize' the Net; to 'infect' the lingua franca; to exchange a different sort of information — mythical, poetical, political, performative, imagistic; and on top of that to find grassroots applications to new technologies and hopefully to do all this with humor and intelligence."[3]

The idea of reconfiguring and rethinking community in cyber terms generated a fair amount of discomfort and disagreement. "Community" was widely thought to be mythologized and abused as a strategic platform. Its elastic and overlapping nature, it was suggested, are rarely taken into account. The absence of physical presence in digital communication presented a roadblock to

165

3
Guillermo Gomez-Peña, "The Virtual Barrio," in *Clicking In: Hot Links to Digital Culture*, ed. Lynn Hershman Leeson (Seattle: Bay Press, 1996),178-79.

Krane

discussing the potential of cyber communities vis-à-vis art practice. The idea of community seemed, for many, essentially tied to felt presence and the sensory body — to shared rituals of comraderie, comfort, and passage. The electronic ether was deemed incapable of fulfilling expectations. "You don't break bread on no Internet," countered Lindsay. Of course, not in the old way. Perhaps that's the point that we should be exploring.

Other recurrent issues included the disturbing conflation of public and private realms in cyberspace; the disembodiment of the Net and its dislocation of time and space, factors that are primary to established rituals of "culture"; the fear of surveillance; and pessimism about the Internet's survival as a two-way forum. (Phil Auslander pointed out that radio and television began as two-way technologies and became one-way technologies with a clear consumer directive.) Periodically, there were quiet reminders that the cyber world should be seen as supplemental, a way to extend rather than supplant aesthetic sensibilities. Can it become, as Mel Chin implied, a means of inserting ideas into transmissions of information and entertainment? Repeatedly, without benefit of response, voices questioned why we want to connect — and about what. "Everyone's talking and no one's listening. Who do I listen to, and why?" said Chin. Obviously, communications technology creates only potentiality, not purpose. "We're not communicating because emotionally we're not communicating," stated Charles Sessoms.

Art is a social mechanism as much as a vehicle for self-expression. Statistics tell us that most people participate in cultural events in groups, with friends or relatives. The luminous computer screen, in contrast, makes for a solitary experience. In spite of the limitless virtual interaction it offers, it is now primarily a conceptual space, commanding focused physical isolation and a certain suspension of ambient stimuli. How will the social context and sensory nature of art transpose? In the inevitable advent of the "post-information" age, will we think in terms of addressing a self-selected and (uncomfortably) invisible audience of one?

The Internet obscures the ability to read identity, a subject that has been valorized at the forefront of artistic practice for a decade now. Initially, we assume that everyone we talk to on the Net is just like us, an egocentric absurdity pointed out by Sessoms. Most Net users are white and male. Yet, as Regina Frank admitted, "I change my personality [on the Net] with each project." Indeed, here identity can be mutable and perpetually reconstituted without accountability, for whatever intent or desire to masquerade. Studies indicate that a significant percentage of males sometimes pose as females in their cyber life. What can we make of this electronic cross-dressing and fluid shapeshifting? Is there new narrative territory herein?

Ostensibly, cyberspace has the potential to plug directly into topical issues of audience and public. It offers an end run around insitutional imperatives, patronage systems, and a mainstream that has swelled to flood level. How wide are we willing to open the doors of art practice? Why are we disinclined to loosen the clinch on routine paradigms of practice, no matter how tired or problematic they may be? Does discussion become polarized in part because we are battle weary and accustomed to taking a position of radicality based on contentiousness rather than vision? Can we begin to imagine a more symbiotic playing field and a catalytic role for art in a very different future? Are the questions of access we trip over really issues of class or are they generational issues? Negroponte ventures: "The haves and have nots are now the young and old."[4] We seem caught in the ricocheting words of an old inner circle. To newly consider art, exhibition, and audience — what we do, how, and for whom — we may first need to expand the parameters of thought to include those who approach visual culture through the back door and are thus redefining the landscape of contemporary life.

4
Negroponte,
Being Digital, 204.

Communications—Guest List

Susan Krane, Director, University of Colorado Art Galleries, Boulder — Session Leader

Philip Auslander, Associate Professor, School of Literature, Communication and Culture, Georgia Institute of Technology, Atlanta

Anne Balsamo, Director of Graduate Studies, School of Literature, Communication and Culture, Georgia Institute of Technology, Atlanta

Cathy Byrd, critic, Atlanta

Mel Chin, professor, School of Art, University of Georgia, Athens, and artist, New York

Monique Curnen, Programming Assistant, Arts Festival of Atlanta

Merrill Elam, Partner, Scogin Elam and Bray Architects, Atlanta

Joyce Fernandes, Program Director, Sculpture Chicago

Regina Frank, artist, Berlin

Adrian King, Corporate Contributions, The Coca-Cola Company, Atlanta

Karen League, Board President, Arts Festival of Atlanta; Principal

and Director of Interior Design, Jova/Daniels/ Busby, Atlanta

Arturo Lindsay, Professor of Art, Spelman College, Atlanta

Darryl Mapp, youth participant, Atlanta

Eric Phelps, Special Audiences, Atlanta

Karen Paluzzi Steele, Managing Director, Sculpture Chicago

Lisa Tuttle, Visual Arts Director, Arts Festival of Atlanta

FRIDAY, AUGUST 30, 6:00 P.M.

Session Leader:

LISA GRAZIOSE CORRIN

Topic:

THE PUBLIC, CONTEMPORARY ART, AND INSTITUTIONS

Location:

THE CASTLE, 87 FIFTEENTH STREET NE

*For this last conversation we returned to
The Castle and to the exhibition "Conversations at The Castle,"
which explored the concept of contemporary art in public space
and researched new modes of communication and
interaction between art, artists,
and the public.*

Method of Preparation:

INTEGRALE

We, as artway of thinking, believe that creative potential is limitless in form, language, and space. Here we limited ingredients to one basic element — the tomato — to inspire maximum creativity from the guests invited to the kitchen. This method underlines creativity as the foundation of art, from which emerges many languages and forms of work. The meal was completed by a very simple dessert — just two ingredients united — but one whose taste is special.

Menu:

PROSECCO PRIMO FRANCO

SUCCO DI POMODORO

GAZPACHO

SPAGHETTI AL POMODORO

CREMA DI POMODORO

INSALATA DI POMODORO

POMODORI RIPIENI

FRAGOLE CON FRAGOLINO

ESSPRESSO ILLY

GRAPPA

LISA GRAZIOSE CORRIN

THE CONTEMPORANEOUS MUSEUM

The critic Arthur C. Danto proposed recently that the art of the past twenty-five years reveals an evolving loss of faith in the Renaissance idea of a progressive narrative of art history. With this loss of faith in what later became the official or "master" narrative of art history, Danto argues, has come the end of the "era of art" in which individuals calling themselves artists created objects that were self-consciously called art for display in special spaces known as museums. We are, writes Danto, "emerging from the era of art into something else, the exact shape and structure of which remains to be understood."[1] The idea that an unforeseen, seismic rupture may be radically shifting the cultural landscape can seem alternately frightening and liberating. While the notion of "rupture" does little to break with a linear model of history, concepts of art, artist, and museum are now more and more commonly viewed as historically relative constructions that cannot be ascribed unified or fixed meanings. This change in consciousness is a disquieting reminder that culture is dynamic and borderless.

In this unsettling landscape, where contemporary art is spoken of largely in terms of ideas and often comes in forms that resist all of our previous assumptions of what art is and how it behaves, how do we view and discuss, let alone display, what contemporary artists do? How do we reconcile the disruption and discontinuity experienced when, after navigating ubiquitous museum neoclassical facades and jewelbox-like Old Master galleries we pass into the sterile, atemporal white cube for modern art, stuck on like an ungainly appendage? These days, to encounter contemporary art is to bring to our looking experience not only a well-focused retina but also skills for relocating what is outside the frame into an expanded field of vision. The theoretical vocabulary used to discuss art is often highly specialized, requiring substantial interdisciplinary resources. A basic knowledge of art history is barely adequate preparation. For the curator, there is the added responsibility of making aesthetic judgments, of discerning the significance of international artistic production, and

1
Arthur C. Danto, *After the End of Art: Contemporary Art and the Pale of History* (Princeton: Princeton University Press, 1997), 2-19.

LISA GRAZIOSE CORRIN is curator at the Serpentine Gallery, London. As chief curator at the Contemporary Museum, Baltimore, from 1989 to 1997, she curated exhibitions in unexpected settings, exploring the relationship between past and present though interdisciplinary collaborations with other museums: "Mining the Museum: An Installation by Fred Wilson" at the Maryland Historical Society; "Going for Baroque: Eighteen Contemporary Artists Fascinated with the Baroque and Rococo" at the Walters Art Gallery; "Can-ton: The Baltimore Series" (by Beijing-born artist Hung Liu) with the Baltimore City Life Museums; "Labor of Love" (by Willie Cole) at the Baltimore Museum of Industry; "Aboard the CyberClipper: A Transatlantic Technological Adventure" with the Goethe Institut, Maryland Public Television, and the Ministry of Culture, Hamburg; and a "phantom exhibition" at the Baltimore Museum of Art. She received a BA in art history from Mary Washington College, Fredericksburg, Virginia; studied at University College, London; completed MA coursework in art history, theory, and criticism at the State University of New York at Stony Brook; and is a PhD candidate in cultural analysis at the University of Amsterdam. Corrin's publications include a monograph on Mark Dion (Phaidon Press, 1997).

knowledge of a burgeoning list of media from painting and sculpture to time-based works such as performance, video, and art on the Internet. It is hardly surprising that even for the most open-minded and curious individual, experiencing contemporary art means readjusting to an elastic language of looking and thinking about what artists do and what objects mean, a task that can seem demanding and daunting. Yet, can there be a more exciting time to be a museum of twentieth- (and soon twenty-first) century culture?

Indeed, this is a time for the emergence of an enlarged language for making, discussing, and exhibiting art, for expanding our concept of what constitutes the terrain of "high art," and for participating in conversations that will give shape to the expansive cultural structure to which Danto refers. With such an expansion, the museum will no longer be reduced to mere artifact. Rather, we may regard it as a living organism that can adapt to the irrepressible flux of the cultural tide. How do we begin the task of re-imagining a living, truly contemporary museum?

The museum, part of whose mission is the preservation of the past, is a fragile filament pulled tautly between the past and future, where the implications of vast social changes can be contemplated and from which relationships to time and to each other can be understood. Perhaps the most accelerated of these changes in the 1990s are technological developments such as the Internet. Despite ongoing discussions about the consequences of economic inequity, these information technologies, like inflated currencies, risk dividing us along new social lines of the information rich and poor, further limiting the ability of human beings to share in an equal conversation about their future. Moreover, this technology can, with the stroke of a button, erase the past by manipulating images and texts. Each day the World Wide Web swallows millions of information bytes, returning them to us the next minute as something irrevocably altered. How far will we go to eschew memory in favor of a technological hygiene system? The implications of such inventions demand that, despite its value-laden spaces and behaviors, we do not sacrifice the museum as a collective, cultural space for asking fundamental questions about what it means to be part of the interconnected web that has characterized human experience of the previous several thousand years and which will continue to weave our lives together.

I believe there is a place in this new cultural landscape for something I will call the "contemporaneous museum," which can serve as a bridge to a perplexed public — including the no less perplexed art world — caught in the fissure of this massive transformation in consciousness. Such a bridge is not very easy to build and requires risk and ingenuity because contemporary culture is rather resistant to discipline. The primary objective of museums since their advent during the Enlightenment has been to discipline the creative enterprise, to bring things into taxonomic order, to subsume information into a prescribed and normalized world view. It has always struck me as ironic that this remains the goal, since we, as curators, present objects believed to embody visual expressions of human experience and emotion that often resist easy classification. If culture is so resistant to discipline, is it futile to call for yet another structure to bring it into line? The contemporaneous museum I have in mind would exploit this restless disposition and present conflict,

170

discontinuity, and flux as eminently desirable features in an entity that is aware that its fate will always be in the balance unless it refuses to succumb to stasis.

Visualize the contemporaneous museum as a structure within a structure, an autonomous entity within the rubric of the existing collecting institution with discrete but complementary activities that may or may not take place within the museum's walls. The contemporaneous museum would have two specific functions. First, it would exhibit the work of living artists in all its pluralism. Second, it would activate the collections with contemporary points-of-view by re-framing objects of the past in fresh, unexpected ways. Objects that are remote from us in time and sentiment would be renewed with a sense of relevance to the present moment. Thus, the museum as repository would continue to flourish as artifact and purveyor/preserver of objects, while a second invisible museum within its structure would work independently and form collaborations internally and externally, changing its shape and redefining itself with each new project. The contemporaneous museum would be not just of the moment but would reflect a sense of the simultaneity of time, of how the layers of time — past, present, and future — accrete on objects, like glistening barnacles on a rock formation.

The contemporaneous museum would begin with four premises. First, it would embrace the necessity of and implicit tension in engaging contemporary culture. Curators currently working within hierarchic, encyclopedic museums often find themselves forced to defend the legitimacy of the study, presentation, and creation of contemporary culture as a serious pursuit. They are frequently confronted by resistance to conjecture or disruption of the practical wisdom that museums, if they want to please "the public," should avoid displaying objects yet to be tarnished by the patina of history. This position dishonors audiences by presuming they are somehow unwilling and deficient in their ability to engage critically with contemporary art by filtering their engagement through their own life experiences.

Thus, the second premise of the contemporaneous museum is that it would assume that the abstract construction called "the public" is in fact a complex and multifaceted group of individuals willing to engage the museum on equal terms. On the cusp of the "era after the end of art," access to contemporary art and ideas will mean a commitment by museums to provide a context for the audience that creates a conversation instead of a lecture. They would invite a diverse and curious public to join with the curatorial voice to define how art keeps a participatory culture vitalized. A new grammar for abstract phrases such as "public" is emerging through projects like "Conversations at The Castle." It is intended to rechart familiar terrain and galvanize discussion, especially outside the art world, and to identify "audience" as a group that does not privilege art world peers. Such projects invite the curator, the artist, and the viewer to question together words like "aesthetics" and "quality" and to ask how we can talk about such terms today. Without first considering how these terms have changed, it is not possible to begin speaking of the future of the museum.

The contemporaneous museum would also view itself as a laboratory and site of debate, where the language of visual culture and its institutions are part of an ongoing evolution in terms. The

171

contemporaneous museum would assume that practice can be the mother of theory. The creative act of producing exhibitions that invite visitors into the arena for conversation would be the basis of the new cultural syntax of which I am speaking. Moreover, the laboratory would not sidestep its obligation to connect what artists do to the wider cultural sphere in which art is made. Notice that the title I use is not the contemporaneous museum *of art*, but the contemporaneous museum. This critical difference announces the intertextuality and interdisciplinary aspects of the museum's positioning of visual culture. Declaring from the outset that its role is to promote conversation, not a particular point of view, it will seek opportunities to explore the connections between visual culture and everyday life with the understanding that the resulting dialogue may raise more questions than answers. By identifying exhibitions as a series of inconclusive experiments, the museum would present "truth" with open-ended circumspection.

The final premise of the contemporaneous museum is that artists would be integral to cultural debate and their relationship to the museum critical to maintaining ongoing viability. If anything characterizes artistic production today, it is pluralism. For example, academic traditions co-exist alongside conceptual practices where the object seems to have "dematerialized." Some of the most significant artists practicing today, although acutely aware of the past, no longer view the creative output of their aesthetic ancestors as something to respond to or react against. Rather, for them, the artist produces nonhierarchical "visual culture," and the past, as it is embodied in the museum, is like an infinite archaeological site where disembodied fragments are unearthed and preserved for what they evoke subjectively without being classified according to a specific value system that maintains a universally accepted definition of "art." The contents of the museum are viewed as an infinitely fascinating compendium of information awaiting sifting and rearranging according to the artist's individual preoccupations and insights. The contemporaneous museum would not try to reconcile any divergent perspectives with its own view of history; disparate viewpoints would coexist in splendid irresolution. Just as the museum would share power with the visitor, so it would encourage artists to participate in the exhibition development process.

In Atlanta, this took place with each project presented. For example, it was a work of art — *Chow for "Conversations on Culture"* — that helped create an environment for ritualizing dialogue and encouraging it to flow informally. This artwork was designed to make conversation a work of art, with the site, participants, and food part of its holistic conception. The "curating" of this work involved intense negotiations between the artists, the curator, the project administrative team, and invited guests so that an environment conducive to relaxed and candid discussion could exist among members of the arts community who do not usually "break bread" together. Such a process would seem to open up a unique kind of space for addressing the challenges of presenting and discussing contemporary art with the public. By adapting traditional processes, expectations, and the language of artist-curator relations, the artist-curator team served the group a larger conception of "conversations" than we might have considered. For example, how had the conversations themselves become the art object?

When I was a child, I found the biblical story of the Tower of Babel very confusing. I couldn't

172

understand why God would get so angry when the Babylonians seemed to be working together so effectively to achieve a common goal. Only when I got older did I come to understand that their goal — to reach heaven — was an act of vanity. There was something frightening to me about the condensation of power achieved when everyone spoke one language and acted in unison. The gift of conversation, an art form composed of verbal ping pong spoken between players, turned out to be God's hedge against the human tendency to seek safety in the relative anonymity of the crowd. A "conversational" presentation of art challenges our positions, and encourages unexpected links and intimate connections to be cultivated.

The institutions of art — museums, galleries, alternative spaces, journals — sometimes seem to me to resemble the Tower of Babel. Public, audience, collaboration, and partnership: the more these terms have been discussed the less they have come to mean. We hardly realize that as we repeat the language of our united purpose, the less effective become our well-intended practices. There is a danger of hiding behind words and being lulled into complacency and isolation. The vanity is in not seeing the dangerous vacuum we might inadvertently be creating.

My imagined contemporaneous museum is intended to reconnect us with the meaning of conversation in order to prevent such a void from developing. We must create opportunities for dialogue before homogeneity turns conversation into a lost art and the museum into just another historical fragment. I do not believe the development of the language of this contemporaneous museum will be easy. But, if nothing else, it will return us to asking fundamental questions about the meaning of our cultural institutions and our place within them. Why and for whom should museums continue to exist? How will they remain relevant and responsive to artists more interested in questioning than making visual products? How will the audience be engaged in this questioning? Where will the museum travel on the "information superhighway" that continues to alter the ways we absorb, disseminate, and define cultural knowledge? Why do we think it is important to be engaged in the making, exhibiting, and teaching of contemporary art? Let us hope that while the conversation continues the answers will never remain the same.

The Public, Contemporary Art, and Institutions — Guest List

Lisa Graziose Corrin, Curator, Serpentine Gallery, London — Session Leader

Jack Becker, Director, Forecast Public Artworks; Editor, *Public Art Review*, St. Paul

Teresa Bramlette, Curator, Nexus Contemporary Art Center, Atlanta

Michael Brenson, critic, New York

Jessica Cusick, Director, Public Art and Urban Design, Cultural Arts Council of Houston

Rebecca DesMarais, Director, Youth Art Connection Gallery/Boys & Girls Clubs of Metro Atlanta

Mauricio Dias, artist, Basel

Nicholas Drake, critic, Charleston

Catherine Fox, art critic, *The Atlanta Journal-Constitution*

Pat Fuller, public art consultant, Patricia Fuller & Associates, Boston

Mary Jane Jacob, Curator, "Conversations at The Castle"

Stefania Mantovani, artist, artway of thinking, Venice

Jennifer McGregor-Cutting, art advisor, Hartford

James Meyer, Professor, Art History, Emory University, Atlanta

Maurice O'Connell, artist, Dublin

Anne Pasternak, Director, Creative Time, New York

Ron Platt, Curator, Southeastern Center for Contemporary Art, Winston-Salem

Patricia Phillips, Chair, Art Department, State University of New York, New Paltz

Carrie Pryzbilla, Curator of Contemporary Art, High Museum of Art, Atlanta

Walter Riedweg, artist, Basel

Chris Scoates, Director, Atlanta College of Art Gallery

Ann Tempkin, Senior Curator, Twentieth-Century Art, The Philadelphia Museum of Art

Federica Thiene, artist, artway of thinking, Venice

Lisa Tuttle, Visual Arts Director, Arts Festival of Atlanta

DESIGN AND TYPE COMPOSITION BY:
Lorraine Wild and Amanda Washburn, Los Angeles

COPYEDITING BY:
Margaret Welsh, Chicago

PRINTING BY:
Dr. Cantz'sche Druckerei, Ostfildern

SEPARATIONS BY:
C + S Repro, Filderstadt

PHOTOGRAPHY CREDITS:
All photographs are by John McWilliams, Atlanta, except for the following:
Michael Siede, Atlanta: 8
Chris Verene, Atlanta: 81–83, 91, 93, 94, 113, 127 (both), 135, 141
(both), 149 (both), 159, 167 (both), back cover
Courtesy of Mauricio Dias and Walter Riedweg, Basel: 92, 95
Courtesy of IRWIN, Ljubljana: 68
Courtesy of Federica Thiene and Stefania Mantovani, Venice: 114–17